PRAISE FOR
The Success Lie

"Janelle Bruland gets right to the heart of entrepreneurial happiness in this book! You won't know true entrepreneurial freedom unless you're living your idea of success, not someone else's. Read this to make sure you're on the path to your biggest future!"

DAN SULLIVAN,
President, The Strategic Coach Inc.

"*The Success Lie* is a book I wish I'd had when I started in business and was running myself on fumes. Very helpful advice for all entrepreneurs and business professionals, particularly women trying to balance it all."

MEL ROBBINS,
Author of award-winning *The 5 Second Rule*

"Insightful ideas wrapped in real-life business stories. Janelle Bruland's success story is an inspiration to business owners."

HAL ELROD,
International best-selling author of *The Miracle Morning*

"*The Success Lie* is a life - transforming book for everyone who has been knocked down in life or has been told that they have to "settle" for leftovers. You can transform your life one simple choice at a time, and this book will show you how!"

TOM ZIGLAR,
CEO of Ziglar, Inc.

"Janelle's journey as an entrepreneur provides powerful insights for any business leader, and *The Success Lie* offers her proven strategy for staying in the game. This is one book you don't want to miss."

MARK COLE,
CEO, The John Maxwell Enterprises

"If you are tired of the hype and looking for a proven process to get unstuck and take back control of your life Janelle Bruland will show you how to get there. Her no-nonsense, super practical lessons are all about empowering you to own your outcomes, regardless of what success means to you."

DAN WALDSCHMIDT,
Best-selling author of *Edgy Conversations*

"*The Success Lie* is something every high-achiever needs to learn as early as possible in life. Janelle Bruland has written a digestible, practical and invaluable tool for anyone who is unafraid to look at their life and choose a better path. A game changer!"

PATRICK LENCIONI,
President, The Table Group; best-selling author of
The Five Dysfunctions of a Team **and** *The Advantage*

"Janelle Bruland is a true pioneer in her field. In *The Success Lie,* Bruland expertly explores the critical balance we all seek, and the potential we all have to define what success really means and how to achieve it. A must read!"

MIKE SIMMS,
Chief Procurement Officer, Microsoft

"*The Success Lie* brilliantly unpacks what is missing in motivational teaching which promises 'success-in-a-box'."

SCOTT HOGLE,
Best-Selling author of *Persuade*

"*The Success Lie* demonstrates how to get off the entrepreneurial rollercoaster. Get ready for a life designed by choice."

STANLEY K. DOOBIN,
President, Harvard Maintenance Inc

"Janelle Bruland is an inspiration! Great book that will change lives!"

SCOTT ALEXANDER,
Author of *Rhinoceros Success*

"*The Success Lie* provides powerful, impactful guidance from one SPARK to another. Its straightforward approach allows anyone to realize the nature of success and how it can be achieved with the right mindset, habits, and approach."

ANGIE MORGAN,
Author of the NY Times bestseller *Spark:*
***How to Lead Yourself and Others to Greater Success* and**
Leading from the Front

"This book is a game changer. *The Success Lie* cuts through the noise and unveils the truth behind success. This book has the power to change you forever."

JEFFREY J. FOX,
Author of *How to Become a Rainmaker*

"It is an immensely inspiring experience to read Janelle's personal journey in this book. Not only does she have an amazing story of resilience, grit, and success, but she has developed a true role model for others to learn from. Janelle's commitment to giving back to the communities is rooted in the deep belief that it is the right thing to do, and now she's found a way to amplify her contribution in the shape of a great book, leaving to all of us a legacy we can consult anytime.

Dr. ILHAM KADRI,
CEO Solvay, Past President, and CEO, Diversey

"*The Success Lie* is both timely and relevant. The author draws upon her lifelong journey of learning, growing and changing to offer credible and keen insights, practical tools, important practices and useful habits to help anyone, regardless of position or profession, live a more purposeful and enduringly successful life. By embodying the book's principles and putting into play actions that reflect them, you will create value not just for yourself but also for those in your network of relationships including family, colleagues, clients and friends."

HENRY S. GIVRAY,
Chairman & Former CEO, *SmithBucklin*

"Loved it! Not many personal development books are so hard to put down! Janelle shares her wisdom gleaned from personal struggles and triumphs, turning it into a clear path for others to apply. Highly recommend *The Success Lie*."

ELLIOTT NEFF,
CEO of *Chess4Life* **& Author of** *A Pawn's Journey: Transforming Lives One Move at a Time*

THE
SUCCESS
LIE

5 Simple Truths to Overcome
Overwhelm and Achieve Peace of Mind

JANELLE BRULAND

FOREWORD BY STEPHEN MR COVEY

Made for Success
PUBLISHING

Made For Success Publishing
P.O. Box 1775 Issaquah, WA 98027
www.MadeForSuccessPublishing.com

Distributed by Made for Success Publishing

Library of Congress Cataloging-in-Publication data

Bruland, Janelle

THE SUCCESS LIE:
5 Simple Truths to Overcome Overwhelm and Achieve Peace of Mind
p. cm.

ISBN: 978-1-64146-355-3 (HDBK)
ISBN: 978-1-64146-361-4 (eBOOK)
LCCN: 2018956064

Contents

Foreword

Utah State University held an inauguration event for the launch of the Stephen R. Covey Leadership Center, a student-focused center housed within the University's Jon M. Huntsman School of Business. I had the opportunity to attend the event, along with my mother, siblings, and other family members. Others in attendance included a wide range of business, community, and academic leaders, as well as students and others. The purpose of this new center is to focus on and develop "principle-centered leaders," drawing upon the teachings and insights of my father. "Principle-centered leadership" is a concept prevalent throughout his work, and the mission Utah State University has undertaken with this initiative truly does honor his legacy.

I was invited to speak at the inauguration, and as you can imagine, I spent a great deal of time pondering my father's life and work. In the process of this preparation, one vital concept continued to rise to the top of my thoughts. The desired outcome of Stephen R. Covey's work was about one main thing: *contribution*.

I believe that idea of contribution is foundational to this very personal book.

I met Janelle Bruland when I was speaking on *The Speed of Trust* at an industry conference several months before writing this foreword. She came up to me after my presentation and told me about the book she was working on. She shared that over the course of her work and life, she had met many individuals who had achieved success only to find it wanting.

While people have many different definitions for what "success" really means to them, if life is a continuum or progression, most tend to place success at the peak. It's the target, the place to get to. When we achieve a measure of that success we tend to feel great joy and satisfaction; when we feel that success slipping away, we often experience frustration, disappointment, and even despair. While this perception of success is certainly useful, as it can draw us forward, it's also incomplete.

One of the things I shared in my remarks at the inauguration event was a model I've seen my father reference many times. He would talk about how we progress in our lives through different stages. For many, the accepted map for the progression of life shows that we begin in "Survival," and from there, progress to "Stability," with the next level being "Success." This isn't necessarily inaccurate, nor is it a bad thing, as it can be motivating, but as those who achieve success ultimately find out, it is simply incomplete. There is a 4th stage, which provides meaning and augments the value of all the others. It is "Significance." The more complete way to look at the progression is that we go from survival to stability, to success, to a life of significance.

If significance is your destination, rather than just success, it changes the way you experience every other stage of life. In the same way that you can experience moments or degrees of success, regardless of where you might be now, you can also experience significance all along the way. The difference is that while success is typically about you, significance is all about *others*.

My work on trust has made this very real for me. I believe that it's trust that makes our world go 'round, and my personal mission is to be a catalyst, along with many others, in helping to bring about a global renaissance of trust. This mission, for me, would be real significance. If my focus were on success, I might measure my progress, or my value, in terms of how many books I've sold, or how many people I've spoken to. While those things are helpful, they would be insufficient incentives to sustain the kind of effort, commitment and preparation demanded by the level of contribution I'm seeking to make. They are also insufficient to overcome the kinds of adversity and challenges that I have both experienced and have yet to encounter in the years to come.

To that point, one of my very favorite parts of this book was a powerful and deeply personal story Janelle shares about overcoming crushing adversity. I won't spoil it for you, but suffice it to say that she didn't overcome it by focusing on what success would look like for her if she did. Frankly, I don't think that would have been enough. Rather, I would submit that the source of her great strength grew out of a concern for others, who were dependent on her, and trusted her. She *had* to come through because of a commitment she had to something greater than herself.

Another theme I love that runs through this book is the idea that we are not bound to a pre-defined track in order to achieve the kind of life we'd like to have. While this might seem obvious as we go day to day, it's deceptively easy to find ourselves doing what Janelle calls "living on automatic" and getting stuck in paths others lay out for us. The reality is that we are all free to choose our own path. In this book, Janelle walks us through hers, and how she has found and continued to live a life of significance. I found many of the things she shared to be relatable and to align with principles I believe in.

In my experience, significance, contribution, and trust are inseparable. Trust is the foundation of all of our relationships and interactions with other people. It is in those connections where we find that, if we've worked to deliberately develop our own credibility, we are in a position to have an extraordinary impact on the lives of others – to lead a life of meaningful and significant contribution.

I am confident you will find Janelle's book to be helpful to you on that journey.

Stephen MR Covey

The New York Times and # 1 *Wall Street Journal* best-selling author of *The Speed of Trust*

Chapter 1

THE TRUTH ABOUT SUCCESS

"The truth is the choice is yours, and yours alone, to live your best life."

Are you living your best life? Do you know what your best life could look like and feel that it's out of reach? Or do you not yet know what that best life looks like? This is a personal question we have to answer for ourselves. The good news is each of us can identify and take steps to achieve a life of joy and significance – one where we are the best version of ourselves and contributing fully to the things that matter most to us.

You have likely picked up this book as you are a high achiever who is constantly looking for ways to improve.

You don't need to be told to work harder, as this comes naturally to you. You have likely had some success in areas and seasons of your life. Perhaps you have even experienced times of major success. At the same time, you have felt the gap – the space between what is and what could be. The gap can be recognized when, despite the amount of success you have had, you still find yourself wanting. You may simply feel something is missing; you feel empty or completely overwhelmed. Or perhaps drained to the point where you are not sure where to turn. It's ok. I have been there too and I can help you.

Over 20 years ago, I started a small services company out of the living room of my home. Today it is a successful regional enterprise that has been recognized as an industry leader. At times over the years as our company has grown, it has been hard to keep a balance between work and home. Working in commercial facility services – an industry that is on the go 24/7 – makes it challenging to stay on top of everything.

As a seasoned entrepreneur I understand well the feeling of being on top of the world one moment with the new client you have won, or product you have launched, and crashing to earth at a lightning pace the next moment when you find the bank account short for payroll, or receive notice from one of your key people that they'll be leaving. It is a rollercoaster of highs and lows – sometimes within a 24-hour period!

And this is just one aspect of your life. Add to it the desire to be present with your family, spend time with friends, and give back to your community. The list goes on, and it can feel like you don't have enough time in the day to do everything you want to do. Or sometimes, it seems like no matter what you are doing, you feel you should be doing something else.

I can relate – when I am traveling for work, I am missing my daughter's basketball game. When I am at her game, I am tempted to check my phone to see what is going on at work. It doesn't matter that the game is at 7 p.m., because that is when most of our teams are working cleaning commercial buildings.

Entrepreneurs and business professionals alike often struggle with juggling too many balls and end up feeling frustrated and overwhelmed trying to keep up in this fast-paced world we live in. Consumed by media and the constant barrage of communications from tweets, texts, TV, radio, and the web, we are on information overload. It seems impossible to keep up.

The worldwide instant access we now have at our fingertips compared to the generations before us is astounding. Did you know that we have access to more information in just one day than our great grandparents had in their entire lifetime? When our grandparents wanted to connect with someone, they had to make the choice to do so – to either call them, write a letter or meet in person. They couldn't just text someone while simultaneously listening to the news, checking Twitter and surfing the web. They maybe got lost a little more without a GPS but let's get real – sometimes Siri gives us the wrong directions. Somehow our grandparents got to where they needed to go; and they survived not knowing instantly about the engagement of a prince, the business tycoon's latest lawsuit, or the earthquake on the other side of the world as it was happening. They found out the information on the nightly news, or in the newspaper the next day. Without all our modern conveniences they seemed to do just fine. Maybe better.

Now in this age of information, we can get our emails on our watches, video-chat with our colleague in Indonesia, and download apps on focus and prioritization. These improvements in technology can be great and they are certainly plentiful. However, because there are so many of them – so many sites providing news alerts, so many apps to choose from, so many educational articles and blogs – we are perpetually at risk of drowning in distraction.

I understand the heavy burden of those who are overwhelmed and exhausted from running on the treadmill society says is the way to success. Work harder, longer, sacrificing everything, even your health or family. If we succumb to what everyone else is doing, we will continue to be overwhelmed.

There is another way to approach this challenge. I have been on this treadmill myself and discovered what I call the "Success Lie." The process of constantly striving day in and day out – even if it ultimately brings crazy success – often leaves one exhausted, unsatisfied and still wanting more. It can damage your health, your relationships and all the things that really matter most. After years of striving, I found myself in a situation where my family was doing well, and I had achieved my dream of building a successful business and yet somehow, despite all of this, I was left feeling somewhat empty and confused. Even with all that I had accomplished, I was left feeling like it wasn't enough. I realized that instead of being in the driver's seat of my life, I had taken a back seat, allowing societal pressures to tell me what mattered.

Once this became clear, I got myself off the treadmill and made the decision to take back my life. You can do it too. But it's not easy. It requires first making a choice. You must realize that the life you are living is not working for you, and is certainly not the one that you were destined to have. Realizing this is incredibly freeing and empowering. Once you've made this discovery, you can then make the choice to move forward and do things differently. You can learn to be intentional with the things that matter, and eliminate everything else.

You can learn to be intentional with the things that matter, and eliminate everything else.

I was compelled to write this book to share with you what I uncovered as the *truths* about success. Consider the following:

- You don't have to stay in the gap – the space between where you find yourself now versus where you want to be. The truth is you can determine what you want your legacy to be and then design the path that takes you there.

- You are not trapped by the circumstances you are in and unable to make changes. The truth is you can decide what is truly important and live by those values and priorities.

- You do not need to fall victim to circumstances and difficulties that will invariably come your way. Instead, with the right perspective, these times can be teachers and instrumental to your growth.

- You do not have to live overworked and overwhelmed. Instead, you can develop success habits and disciplines to take you to peak performance. By implementing these tools you will have more energy, work less and achieve more.

- You may think you don't have the power to remove personal barriers. The truth is you can learn what is getting in the way of your success, and take steps to increase your self-awareness, improve your skills, and become a better leader of yourself and others.

Above all the truth is the choice is yours, and yours alone to live your best life – the life of significance you were always meant to live. Throughout the pages of this book, I will take you along my journey through the highs and lows of being an entrepreneur, and the lessons learned along the way. I will share with you a proven strategy to let go of the modern world's path to success and instead create a life of fulfillment and true significance. Only when living such a life are you aligned in your values, living your purpose, loving your work, and positively impacting your family and community.

You can choose to read this book and set it aside as having some nice ideas and concepts. But if you do, your life will remain unchanged. Why not make a better choice; one that has the power to be life transforming? Why not choose to follow the roadmap, do the work, and gain control of your life? If you do, all kinds of possibilities will open up to you.

Imagine yourself creating and then living the life you have always wanted. Picture living a life that is unapologetically bold and authentically you, in which you spend your days doing what you are designed to do and loving it. Imagine living a life of significance.

This is true success. Let's get started.

TRANSFORM YOUR LIFE

SECTION ONE

Chapter 2

EVERYTHING IS A CHOICE

"No matter what circumstances you face, it is always your choice to respond in a way that will lead you forward."

Although it may not seem like it, and at times can be easy to argue the opposite, everything is a choice. Often it is easier to see the reason for something happening as outside forces causing things to occur in our lives, rather than the result of a choice we have made. There are so many circumstances in this world that are bigger than us and beyond our control, put into place by systems we have no way of regulating or changing. Situations frequently occur that we did not expect or plan for. Being caught by surprise might make an experience more upsetting, but that does not mean we are helpless and unable to choose a positive response. Quite the contrary, first we choose how we react to our circumstances, then we choose to move forward or stay stuck where we are.

Are you choosing optimism or pessimism? Are you geared more toward tenacity or hesitancy? Are you opting for an approach that stresses life-long learning, giving-back, and being community minded or a head-in-the-sand, self-centered perspective?

These all represent choices that are made in big and small ways every day. It is beneficial to choose actions and behaviors that promote positivity. A conscious decision to maintain an optimistic mindset regardless of circumstances is one of those choices I made early in my career. In this chapter you will learn about how everything is a choice and sometimes we choose to let others impact us positively or negatively, but ultimately the choice is ours.

It Started with One Small Choice

In 1995, I began a business journey that has changed my life. Nine months pregnant with my second child, I made the small yet significant choice to become an entrepreneur.

The grind of several years working in management in another field, I wanted a career that offered scheduling flexibility so

I could spend time with my young children, and allow me to give back to my community. It was that quest that led me to start a contract cleaning company. Although I knew this choice would present its challenges, I thought owning a small business would be a great side investment while allowing me to be a mom.

And so, Management Services Northwest (MSNW) began in a small office in the upstairs landing of my home, with a handful of employees. I remember having my small team over to our home for breakfast and our first staff meeting. I knew little about the janitorial industry at the time and admitted it to them. But I did let them know I was excited to learn, looked forward to their help, and together we were going to take great care of our clients and grow a successful business.

Recognizing that strong relationships were the foundation, I made a commitment to work closely with the team and provide the resources they needed to take excellent care of our accounts. I believed if our customers were happy they would refer us to other businesses and we would grow.

Similar to the startup stories of other emerging businesses, I ran MSNW out of my home and operated it from there for many years while my children were young. I managed all aspects of the business from my home base holding team meetings, taking client calls, and warehousing supplies and equipment. In the beginning I wore a number of hats from sales person to receptionist, chief strategist to accountant.

By maintaining our commitment to quality service promised during my very first team meeting, we steadily grew the business.

As our clients' businesses grew, MSNW grew with them, both geographically and in the scope of services we offered. MSNW evolved from a strictly janitorial service operation serving a small county in Washington state to a full-scale facility management company serving throughout the Pacific Northwest. As clients requested new services, such as landscaping or snow removal, we added those specialists to our team as they made sense financially for the business.

We operate by the slogan "We'll take care of it," that drives everything we do, from our company culture to client services and community involvement. Our unique advantage is that we are a one call source for all facility services from janitorial and landscaping, to complete facility management. Because we bundle services such as plumbing, electrical, landscaping, janitorial, etc. we are able to create efficiencies, increase the quality of the services, and free our clients to focus on their important work.

As founder and CEO, I have been privileged and humbled to see MSNW grow from a small start up into a thriving regional enterprise and one of the largest facility service providers in the Pacific Northwest with over 450 employees and multiple service partners. With year over year double digit growth, our company has been named as one of the fastest growing companies by *Inc. Magazine* and *Puget Sound Business Journal.*

The choice to start my own business was not without challenges. I knew full well the statistics were against me - according to the Small Business Administration, 80% of small businesses fail in the first year. Regardless, I was determined to beat the odds. Thankfully, with the support of passionate, dedicated team members and wonderful client partners we have not only kept our doors open for over two decades, but created a successful, sustainable business that is making a positive impact.

Being an entrepreneur is an exhilarating and challenging adventure, and as mentioned in the last chapter, a roller-coaster of highs and lows. I have made mistakes and learned many valuable lessons along the way. Through it all I learned to think beyond the narrow bounds of a successful career to a significant life. I developed the Leader's Success Plan provided at the end of the book, which is a proven system you can follow to design a life of purpose and significance. There is no silver bullet, and the path is not always easy, but it is well worth it. Let me help you uncover the truths that have held you back, and transform your life to the one you have always dreamed of, one simple choice at a time.

Choose Your Response

I have often been asked how I have been successful in life and business, especially making it through the deep recession, when many companies failed. I have found that the secret of continued progress is due to two responses used repeatedly through the good and especially the challenging times of my life.

My first response to challenges is a natural tendency toward optimism. This optimism is something I can summon in any given situation and reflects my general perception of life as a "cup half full" versus "half empty." The second response is one of tenacity; I tend to choose to never give up, no matter what happens. When you fall down, or are even kicked down, you always get back up, put one foot in front of the other and keep going.

My optimism and tenacity were challenged on a number of occasions. I went through my own personal trauma years ago when I suddenly found myself a single mother to my three daughters.

During this time, I could have given up and certainly wanted to at times. I had a choice to make. Was I going to let this troubling situation paralyze me or would I persevere through the struggles? It was difficult, but I made the decision that I was going to be the best parent I could be, the best employer, and have the best business.

I read a very helpful book at the time by Larry Wilson called *Play to Win*. In it, he describes two kinds of people:

1. "Playing not to lose: Avoiding situations where we might lose, fail, be emotionally hurt, or be rejected.[1]
2. Playing to win: Consciously choosing to go as far as we can with all that we have and learning from whatever happens."[2]

Most people like to face life by playing not to lose, by doing everything they can to play it safe. Those who take the road less traveled are playing to win. With this mindset, I cannot fail. I can only learn and grow!

Listen to Your Own Voice

I was a single mother for many years. My family has always been my primary purpose, with my business pursuits coming second. However, the heavy responsibility of supporting my family completely on my own, as well as the responsibility of leading a growing company was especially daunting during this challenging time.

I decided to meet with an industry consultant whom I respected. I told him of the importance to me of being a good parent first and shared my thoughts of working less than full time, as well as my plans to continue to grow my business successfully to the next level. He told me, "You will not be able to continue the positive upward trend you have experienced working less than full time. You need to commit to working 40 hours plus per week – or more like 50 to 60 hours – to accomplish your goals."

My best decision was to not listen to that consultant's advice. Instead, I became even more committed to my part-time work week. In fact, I decided to schedule myself completely out of the office one day of the week. In the next two years, my business grew more than 130 percent. More importantly, because of the decision to work part time, my children grew up with a mom who didn't miss the important events in their lives, took the time to volunteer for their school activities, and provided an example of what it can mean to be successful at work and at home.

Choose Your Mindset

My optimism and tenacity were not just challenged in my personal life but in business too. One of the most challenging times for our business was when the Great Recession hit. Overnight, our world changed drastically. I observed several clients struggle financially, and one client partner of over 13 years was shut down by the FDIC. There was a spirit of fear around us. Many of my staff had spouses or family members who had lost jobs or businesses, and our own project division dropped 30% overnight. It was a scary time to be a business owner. I have to admit there were some sleepless nights worrying about providing for all of the families who called MSNW home. I remember one moment when it seemed things were crashing down around us, and I too, allowed myself to become paralyzed by fear. One of my managers pulled me aside and said to me, "Janelle, you are always the one that puts the wind in our sails, but you can also take it out."

That was a wake-up call for me. I made the fundamental decision that day to do whatever it took to thrive in the down economy, to learn whatever lessons we could as a company and use them to prepare for a great future.

This type of mindset is a choice. It's a choice that takes work and means not looking at problems as insurmountable, but rather as opportunities. Dr. Carol Dweck, in her book *Mindset,* calls this approach a "growth mindset" versus "a fixed mindset." A fixed mindset is where one identifies themselves as someone who cannot change; one who feels labeled by their failures; and gets quickly discouraged when things become hard. On the other hand, a growth mindset is one, as I have described, where every difficulty provides an opportunity to learn and take yourself forward.[3] Dweck says, "You have a choice. Mindsets are just beliefs. They're powerful beliefs, but they're just something in your mind, and you can change your mind."[4]

It's a choice that takes work and means not looking at problems as insurmountable, but rather as opportunities.

By choosing this growth mindset, you seek to constantly find a way to move forward towards positive solutions. Sometimes it's not easy. There were days I felt deflated and wondered how I would go into the office and face our team when I knew the challenges ahead. Again, what I had to do was make the choice to not allow myself to wallow in self-pity and to instead move forward in confidence. Trusting my business, employees and clients was also a choice. All of these small choices, made day after day, slowly brought us through the worst of it.

Once I had stopped listening to outside forces and committed to the positive continued success of my business, I began to act in a way that supported the choices that I had made. This impacted the entire team, encouraging them to make their own choices about attitude and commitment. We even talked about how we put on our company uniform in a different way. Similar to a team member working at Disneyland who puts on the princess costume and becomes a princess, we can leave our situations behind when we come to work as soon as we put on our costume. No matter what challenge was being faced at home; I encouraged them to believe that when they came into work and put on the MSNW logo shirt, they became MSNW. That shirt means you're positive, you're passionate, and you're going to have a really great day. It was actually a very helpful reminder that way – both simple, yet tangible.

Every reaction, interaction and
conversation is a choice for the future.

This example is poignant to me as it was a stark reminder that we live life based on our own design. From then on it was clear that every reaction, interaction and conversation was a choice for the future. At the time we were in an office space that we had significantly outgrown. Our human resources manager didn't even have an office door. While everyone was saying, "hunker down," "wait for everything to blow over," "hold on to your money," I purchased a new office for our company that was twice the size of the one we were in. This bold move helped to position us for further growth. Because of that decision we were able to take on a regional contract the following year which led to our strongest year in company history.

No matter what circumstances you face, it is always your choice to respond in a way that will lead you forward.

PLAYING TO WIN

Reflect on circumstances in your own life and your typical response, and answer the following questions:

1. Is your tendency to "play not to lose" or do you typically "play to win?"

2. Is there an area in your life right now where you need to step out of your comfort zone and do something differently? What action could you take?

Listen to Your Own Voice. We are ultimately responsible for our own choices. We often allow others significant power over our decisions. While it is important to seek the counsel of those we trust, consider whether you are allowing the influence of others to impact the way you are living your life more than you should.

CHOOSE YOUR MINDSET

Do you consider yourself an optimistic person by nature, or do you tend to have a pessimistic outlook?

Reflect back on a circumstance that occurred or news that was provided to you within the last year that was not your desired outcome, and answer the following questions:

1. Describe the situation and your initial response. Was your reaction to the situation positive or negative?

2. How did your behavior in the situation impact others? In other words, did your actions elicit a positive or negative response in those around you?

3. If your reaction and response was not one with a positive mindset, how would you choose to respond differently next time?

Chapter 3

LIVING ON AUTOMATIC

"Automatic living may take us to a place
we never would have chosen to go."

My husband Graham and I enjoy kayaking together on the ocean near our home in Birch Bay. There is nothing more beautiful than being out on the water on a warm summer evening as the sunlight shimmers on the ocean while making its descent. On most days you can watch the sun go down all the way until it appears to hit the water and disappear under the waves, sending colorful pink and purple tones across the sky. I have to admit my typical preference is to spend a lot more time gazing then paddling so it becomes more of a sunset experience than exercise, but that is just fine with me. It is easy to get mesmerized by the beauty of the ocean and forget to watch the tides. On more than one occasion when I stopped paying attention to where I was going, the pulling tides have grabbed the kayak and started carrying me out to sea. I would end up being much further off shore than I ever planned to be.

Our lives can be compared to this kayak experience. It is so common to get caught up in the busyness of life – running a company, raising a family, making time for friends, being involved in your community, and all of the demands this puts on us, that we stop really paying attention to where we're going. Sometimes it happens quickly, but more often gradually, and we wake up one day in a place we never intended to be. We didn't mean to gain the 30 pounds; it came through habits that formed automatically over many years. We never intended to end up in an estranged relationship or divorce. It happened through small decisions, where the most important person in our lives was put in the back seat and other things moved to the forefront. We wanted to be there for all of the growing up moments of our kids, but work got in the way and now they are graduating.

In many areas of our lives, we were just cruising along automatically, and 20 – 30 years later found ourselves in completely different places than where we ever wanted to be.

To illustrate how much even the smallest misstep can have a large effect over time, let's look at flying an airplane, where precision is an absolute must. Here are some interesting stats about flying *just one degree* off course:

1. For every degree you fly off course, you will miss your target by 92 feet for every mile that you fly.
2. For every 60 miles you fly, you will miss your target by one mile.
3. When flying from JFK to LAX it will put you nearly 50 miles away from your destination.
4. When flying around the equator you will land almost 500 miles off target.[5]

A one-degree mistake may not seem like a big deal, but when you can see the potential of the enormous impact, it causes you to pay attention. Though you may have tolerated automatic living in the past, becoming aware of it and realizing how easy it is to get off course will make you more attentive to your actions going forward.

Choose to be Intentional

Instead of living on automatic, we can choose intentional living.

In the services company I lead, one of our core values is continuous improvement in everything we do. In order to improve, there must be growth. At times throughout our 23 years of business, growing our people and our company seemed easy, almost automatic. However, looking back it wasn't automatic, but a result of intentional effort.

John Maxwell, in his book *The 15 Invaluable Laws of Growth*, reminds us of the need for intentionality in order to improve. "When we are children, our bodies grow automatically. A year goes by, and we become taller, stronger, and more capable of doing new things and facing new challenges. I think many people carry into adulthood a subconscious belief that mental, spiritual, and emotional growth follows a similar pattern. Time goes by, and we simply get better."[6]

> Individuals don't improve automatically, and companies don't improve automatically. They improve only as the result of intentional effort.

This is not the case. Individuals don't improve automatically, and companies don't improve automatically. They improve only as the result of intentional effort. In my business, matching our core value of continuous improvement, we seek team members with a passion for learning and growth, and commit to providing training opportunities to ensure they are constantly growing. We are intentional about regularly evaluating our company performance.

Through evaluation processes such as a company SWOT (a brainstorming session where your team lists strengths, weaknesses, opportunities and threats), we identify areas for improvement, then develop a strategy and goals to keep moving the company forward.

Without the same level of intentionality in our personal lives, we can drift backward rather than improve and grow.

Much of our Behavior is Unconscious

Sigmund Freud, the Austrian neurologist and founder of psychoanalysis in the early 1900s, thoroughly explored the human mind and was one of the first scholars to talk about the power of the conscious and unconscious.[7] According to Freud's model, the unconscious mind is the primary guiding influence over daily life and leads to the most common of our human behaviors. It is far more powerful than the conscious mind, which consists of all of the mental processes of which we are aware.

Living on automatic is the result of this unconscious behavior, which will eventually lead to the habits or routines that control much of what we do.

Living on automatic is the result of this unconscious behavior, which will eventually lead to the habits or routines that control much of what we do. Whenever we do something over and over again, eventually it will be something that we do with ease, and without giving it much thought. As an example, think about your drive home from work every day. As creatures of habit, we will likely take the very same route home day after day without giving it any thought. When I moved to a different house in my town, there were several times over the first few weeks where I found myself ending up on the street at my old address.

Have you ever rearranged the drawers in your kitchen and found yourself going to the old silverware drawer about ten times until you finally trained your brain as to where the new drawer is? You get the idea.

These automatic behaviors result in habits which can either be good habits or more often, bad habits that lead us over time to the places we don't want to go and the life we don't want to lead. We will talk more about how to establish good habits and routines later in the book.

Identify Where You are Living on Automatic

There are seven main areas of life that you need to focus on and bring together in order to grow and reach your maximum potential.

They are:

- Physical – Your Health

- Mental – Your Mind, Personal Growth

- Spiritual – Your Values

- Family & Friends – Your Relationships

- Career/Business – Your Professional Life

- Financial – Your Money

- Fun & Recreation – Your Hobbies

Zig Ziglar, well known for Ziglar's *Wheel of Life*, speaks about the main areas of your life as spokes on a wheel. Most of the "bumps" we experience in life are not due to the road, but the lack of attention to certain areas in our life which can make us off balance.

Think of each of these life areas as a place on the wheel. Together they make up a circle of your life. As you review each of these, where do you find your wheel full and round, and what areas need some help? A Life Wheel Exercise is included at the end of this chapter. Take time to utilize this effective tool to help you evaluate the 7 main areas of your life.

1. Physical

This area of your life focuses on your health and well-being. We only have one body and when it is not properly cared for, it can affect all of the other areas of our life. Yet, it is one of the top areas that is neglected. Like a car that needs to be regularly fueled and maintained to function properly, so do our bodies, or they will break down.

2. Mental

This area of your life focuses on the state of your mind as well as your personal growth. What are you doing to learn and grow? As we highlighted earlier in the chapter, mental growth does not happen automatically but as a result of intentional effort.

Entrepreneurs, CEOs and executives often find themselves so focused on growing and developing their teams, that they stop taking the time to develop themselves. When is the last time you took time out for yourself to take a class to improve on a skill, or learn something new?

3. Spiritual

This area of your life is your "Why." I believe we were created on purpose, for a purpose, and each of us needs to determine what that is. This begins with identifying your personal values – what is most important to you. We will talk more about the importance of our personal values in Chapter 5 – The Juggling Act. Often, we fall into the trap of living for someone else's values – perhaps our parents, a significant other, or a boss. When we are not sure of and living true to our own values, this will result in a sense of lacking in this area of your life.

For me, my faith has been an integral part of my life, has given me direction, and carried me through the difficult times. There have been situations where I didn't know how I would have made it were it not for this beacon keeping me centered.

4. Family & Friends

The relationships in our lives are so important to experience full and abundant living. This is also an area in which it is easy to coast on automatic and not realize the significance our relationships have on the trajectory of our lives. Jim Rohn said it well, "You are the average of the five people you spend the most time with." Are you spending time with people that lift you up, encourage you, and challenge you? Do they share your values and live a life you admire? Or are the main people you spend regular time with pulling you down and holding you back?

A great exercise is to get these relationships on paper and evaluate them one by one. As you look back over the last month, or last year, list the three to five individuals that you spend the most time with (in order of most time spent) personally, professionally, and socially. Once you have done this, review each name and ask yourself, Does this individual bring me up or bring me down?" Another way to look at it is after spending time with this individual do you leave the situation feeling better, more energized, and happy, or do you leave feeling uneasy, disappointed, and drained?

Once you have the list and have evaluated it, the next step is to determine if you should expand the relationship, create limits or boundaries around it, or end it altogether. Sometimes the toughest decision to make is to end a relationship that is harming you, but it will make an incredible difference in your life. Just because you have had that friend since grade school, doesn't mean you have to keep them when they are not a positive and uplifting influence in your life. Remember, don't walk with the wild, the broken, or the broke. This doesn't mean you can't support these people in your life. You just don't want them in your inner circle.

5. Career/Business

This is such an important category for most of us, in fact, one that we too often perceive as being our main identity. Think of the most common question people ask when greeting others at a business event: "What do you do?"

For me, I have to guard this area of my life very carefully. Like many driven executives who are "all in" when it comes to growing our businesses, it is easy to get consumed with our businesses and careers to the detriment of the other important areas of life.

When it comes to your career, are you doing what you love and loving what you do? If an immediate YES doesn't come to mind, this category is worth further study. We spend far too much time working to be in a place of work or type of work that is not suited to our unique passion, gifts and talents.

6. Financial

Our financial state is another area that easily slips into automatic, and where small, seemingly insignificant decisions can lead to large negative results over time. As you evaluate this area, ask yourself if you are comfortable with your current financial situation and plan for the future, or if this is an area in your life that creates anxiety, or sleepless nights.

If the latter is the case, simple money management tools can help get us on the right path and lead us to more secure financial futures.

7. Fun & Recreation

For many, taking the time for personal fun and recreation is last on the list, and often gets eliminated altogether due to so many demands in the other life areas.

Talk to a typical business owner or executive and they will tell you that they are working long and hard on their career goals and haven't taken a real vacation in years, if ever. When they do, they don't truly unplug as they feel it is necessary to stay connected with the office.

Society has made us feel guilty for taking time off, so much so that we wear a badge of honor for working the most hours of anyone else on the team. Think about the standard company handbook, where you earn vacation as a reward after a year of service. When it comes time to take it, there often seems to be so much work to do that it is not worth it to take the time off.

Declare time for rejuvenation. We have to fight against the part of our work ethic that tells us time off equals "slacker," when it simply is not true. Research shows that downtime replenishes the brain's stores of attention and motivation, enhances productivity and creativity, and is essential to achieve our highest levels of performance. When we take the time to rest, our brains are anything but idle. Instead downtime gives the brain an opportunity to make sense of the day and what it has recently learned; to surface unresolved tension; and to move from the external world to reflect within. [8]

I will talk more about how we can train our brains for better focus later in the book. The bottom line is that all of us need to take proper time for rest and rejuvenation in order to operate at our optimum levels.

In order to transition to intentional living, and the full and abundant life we desire, we need to first understand where in our lives the unconscious, automatic living is hurting us. Then we can learn how to break the pattern and wake up, if you will. Once we're awake, we can decide to live intentionally.

AUTOMATIC LIVING

As you think about your own life, answer the following questions:

1. In what areas are you running on automatic? Identify two to three gaps in your life where automatic living has held you back from where you want to be.

2. What kind of results has that automatic living produced?

3. Where would making a change have the potential to transform your life?

THE 7 LIFE AREAS WHEEL

Think of the 7 main areas of life described in this chapter as spokes on a wheel. On a scale of 1-10, 10 being best, evaluate the condition of each of these areas and chart it on the graph below. Then connect the dots around the circle. Where is your wheel full and round, and what areas need some help?

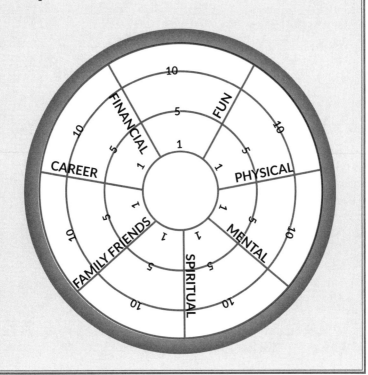

Chapter 4

START WITH THE END IN MIND

"The place God calls you to is the place where your deep gladness and the world's deep hunger meet." Frederick Buechner

---

"All of us get just one exciting life to live here on this earth. How are we going to use it?" This was our speaker, Adria Libolt's opening remark at my daughter's graduation from high school. Although she was making a difference as a teacher, Adria felt called to another vocation as a Deputy Warden in the Michigan Department of Corrections, where she spent over 20 years in prisons. The concept of *how are you going to use your life* is certainly an important question for a high school senior to consider as they are making plans for their futures, but what about the rest of us?

I believe that we are here on earth for a purpose. Each of us has different gifts and talents, and when used to our greatest potential, these gifts will provide excitement and joy to our lives and to others around us. A recent statistic in *Forbes Magazine* stated that 74% of employees are dissatisfied with their work. If we are unhappy with where we currently stand in life, at work or at home, isn't it only us who can make the choice to change it?

As we hire employees to join our team at MSNW, we seek those with the skills to do the work, but even more so, we seek the passion around the work. When we find the individual that loves what they do and is also very good at it, we are confident we have made a successful match.

Whatever stage we are at in life – a recent graduate, a busy Mom managing a household, in the height of a career, or enjoying retirement – we have an opportunity to provide great influence.

Whatever stage we are at in life – a recent graduate, a busy mom managing a household, in the height of a career, or enjoying retirement – we have an opportunity to provide great influence. This influence can be negative and destructive, or positive and life-building. It's crucial to ask ourselves if we are making the choice to live our lives in such a way that we can have the most positive impact on our families and friends, our work, and our communities. The impact we leave over a lifetime becomes our legacy.

The impact we leave over a
lifetime becomes our legacy.

Living a Legacy

At a recent leadership retreat I led, our focus topic was *The Leader's Legacy*. We discussed as a group that all of us want to leave a meaningful legacy – a positive impact on our family, our business, and our community.

The word legacy is defined as follows:

> **legacy, <u>noun</u> , leg·a·cy**
> 1. A gift or a bequest, which is handed down, endowed or conveyed from one person to another.
> 2. Something transmitted from an ancestor or predecessor or from the past.

One of our members approached the topic in a different way. While the rest of us were thinking about the legacy we want to *leave*, which is certainly important, he reminded us of the definition of legacy, and that it starts with something we have been given. All of us have received a legacy *first*. It may be a positive legacy that has been passed on to us, perhaps a special gift, or the traditions that we carry on; or it can be negative – like a behavior propensity, or a problem that exists because of something that has happened in the past. We are then a conduit to pass on the legacy that we create to those who follow us.

A colleague of mine gave the group three key mantras to think about in regard to legacy.

- **Choose It**. Choose today what you want your legacy to be. None of us know how long our lives will be, so we must choose now.

- **Live it**. Live your legacy today. Once you have determined what you want your legacy to be, don't wait. Live it now.

- **Celebrate It**. There is so much to be grateful for. Celebrate the legacy you have received and the legacy you want to live and leave. Find the good in each day.[9]

Start with the End in Mind

You don't want to have regrets. When you ask people at the end of their lives what is most important, they rarely say that it is the fancy car, or the trophies that sit dusty on the shelf. Rather, it is the relationships they have, the loves in their life, the gifts they have given to others. If this type of clarity is gained by people at the end of life, what is it that we can learn from their wisdom?

Palliative care nurse Bronnie Ware took note after spending years with individuals during their last days and ended up writing a book about it titled *The Top Five Regrets of the Dying*.[10] When asking about any regrets her clients had or if there was anything they would do differently she found common themes surfacing. Here are the top five regrets she heard over and over:

1. **"I wish I'd had the courage to live a life true to myself, not the life others expected of me."**[11]

   Ware found this to be the most common regret of all of them, as well as the one that seemed to cause the most frustration as her client's realizations came too late.[12] Are you living a life that is true to yourself? If this is not clear to you, you will have a chance to discover the answer as you work through the next couple of chapters.

2. **"I wish I hadn't worked so hard."**[13]

   I have to admit to struggling with this one when I read this research – perhaps because it needs my attention. A strong work ethic is an admirable thing. I recall my parents showing my siblings and I a good example of working hard and teaching us to do the same - a principle I now teach my own children. The problem comes when work becomes all-consuming and supersedes everything else in your life.

3. **"I wish I'd had the courage to express my feelings."**[14]

So often we allow fears to hold us back. Many people keep things inside in order to "keep the peace" with others. However, when this is done too often you lose part of yourself, along with the ability to truly become everything you are capable of and live the life you are meant to have.

4. **"I wish I had stayed in touch with my friends."**[15]

Loving relationships are the key to a rich and fulfilled life. In the last chapter we talked about friends and family as one of the seven main areas of life. This is an area where we can fall into automatic living and take for granted these important relationships.

5. **"I wish I had let myself be happier."**[16]

You may believe you don't have the power to make your own path. Together we are uncovering this lie and you will discover that happiness is a choice. You don't have to remain stuck in old patterns and habits – instead you can break free to the life you have always wanted.

As you review this list, what is the greatest regret you have as you look over the life you have lived so far? Is one of these a particular "watch" area for you? Take a moment to think about it and write it down.

One of the most difficult, yet most useful exercises I have ever done was writing my own eulogy. Starting with the end in mind, I wrote what I wanted people to remember about me when my life on earth was done. What legacy did I want to leave? What impact did I want to have on the world around me? What would I want those who knew me to say about what I had done with my life? Though understandably a bit morbid, taking the time to do a similar exercise for yourself will be most helpful in determining what you need to be doing now.

Look ahead and think about yourself at the age of 100. As your 100-year-old self, what would you say about the life you are living? In the challenge section at the end of the chapter I have provided some questions to ask yourself. Think about this now, so you don't get to 100 and look back at your life with regret.

I developed a Legacy Timeline exercise that is a helpful tool to review the decades of your life so far – the significant events, the various seasons, the highs and lows, and how they have shaped you into the person you are today. Once you go through the process of filling out the timeline, you then go back and review the last few decades. How have your life experiences impacted you and others and shaped your legacy?

The second part of the timeline exercise is to go forward into the next two decades – a 20-year outlook. What do you want to add to the timeline? Think about and write down what you wish to intentionally create in the coming season to begin fulfilling the legacy you want to leave.

As we come to the end of this chapter, let me leave you with some personal thoughts on this topic of legacy from my esteemed colleagues:

- I will give more and take less.
- I will speak into the lives of others.
- I will ask myself, "What is the right thing to do?"
- Each one of us has more impact than we realize.
- If you are doing the right thing, the legacy part will take care of itself.

The decision is yours. You can continue to live on automatic and take things as they come, or you can choose to live intentionally. Take charge and design your best life – one that is destined to leave a positive legacy. It's up to you. No one can do it for you. Let's make the most out of the one exciting life that we have.

EVALUATE REGRETS

Review the list of regrets in this chapter and answer the following questions:

1. What's your greatest regret as you look over the life you have lived so far?

2. What do you want to change so this is no longer an issue for you? Take a moment to write it down.

3. Of the five top regrets listed, what are one or two that resonate the most for you as an area you need to watch?

Challenge Exercise

START WITH THE END

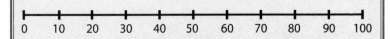

Look ahead and imagine your life as your 100-year-old self. Take the time to answer the following questions:

- As you look back on your many years of living, what have been your most meaningful experiences?

- What have you accomplished that makes you most proud?

- What legacy are you leaving for your children? For this world?

- What do you want others to say about you when you leave this earth? They will either say positive things, negative things, or have nothing to say at all.

Taking the time for this exercise will help you determine the choices you want to make now so you won't ever have to look back with regret later.

Chapter 5

THE JUGGLING ACT

"Today I will focus on the important,
and not allow myself to be
kidnapped by the urgent."

E arlier this year my family and I visited beautiful Victoria, British Columbia to enjoy the world-famous Buskers Festival. The weather was warm, and the atmosphere surreal as we enjoyed the sights and sounds of the famous Inner Harbor with the majestic Parliament Buildings, Royal BC Museum, and the enchanting Empress Hotel – a grand structure built in 1908 with lush green ivy trailing the stone walls, and traditional afternoon tea being served in their elegant foyer. The walkways along the waterfront were filled with street performers from all over the world who mesmerized us with their comedy shows and juggling acts, and their daring feats, from balancing atop high poles to fire throwing.

As leaders in fast paced businesses going seven days a week, we can often feel like street performers juggling several balls at once. We have gotten quite savvy at the juggling, but it takes extreme focus and energy to continue with this balancing act, and we fear any moment we may not just drop one ball but several.

Does this sound familiar? A business speaker I listened to some time ago asked if we were allowing ourselves to be "kidnapped by the urgent." This phrase has stuck with me as it is so fitting. How often do we get to the end of our work day and find that we didn't accomplish what we had hoped as we found ourselves constantly interrupted with what seemed to be urgent matters? If we take the time to look back at these activities that seemed so urgent at the time, most often we find they really weren't the emergencies they seemed to be and could have waited their place behind the important things that needed our attention.

Identify your "Why"

Often, the difficult thing is determining what is truly important. As described in the main areas of your life in chapter two, each of us must take the time to identify our "Whys." In other words, what is your purpose in life? What are your personal values? What is most important to you?

Parker Palmer, in his book *Let Your Life Speak*, ponders the course of his life and describes his path to discovering his own purpose. In order to have our lives mean something he urges that we listen for the voice of vocation to discover what it is our life is supposed to represent. He says, "Vocation does not come from willfulness. It comes from listening. I must listen to my life and try to understand what it is truly about, quite apart from what I would like it to be about-or my life will never represent anything real in the world, no matter how earnest my intentions. That insight is hidden in the word vocation itself, which is rooted in the Latin for "voice." Vocation does not mean a goal that I pursue. It means a calling that I hear.

Before I can tell my life what I want to do with it, I must listen to my life telling me who I am. I must listen for the truths and values at the heart of my own identity, not the standards by which I must live, but the standards by which I cannot help but live if I am living my own life."[17]

To live your own life then, one of purpose and intention, you must first determine what your values are.

There is a difference between values and priorities. You cannot decide what your priorities are without having values. A priority is something that is important and that you would choose to work on before other things. A value, on the other hand, describes who you are. Values are the guidelines and beliefs a person uses when confronted with a situation in which a choice is made. They do not change from situation to situation and typically no amount of external influence will affect them. Look behind one's behavior and you will likely uncover the values behind them.

> **val·ue**, /valyoo̅/
>
> a person's principles or standards of behavior; one's judgment of what is important in life.
>
> "they internalize their parents' rules and values"
>
> **synonyms:** principles, ethics, moral code, morals, standards, code of behavior.

Much of the value system created in my own life was instilled as I was growing up. It wasn't that my parents were ever really saying things about what their values and priorities were, but it was the example of their lives and how they lived that left a lasting impression.

Look behind one's behavior and you will likely **uncover the values behind them.**

I was born in the beautiful Pacific Northwest, grew up in the small town of Lynden, Washington, and still am a part of the community today. Lynden, with a population of 3,000 in my childhood years, was the typical, traditional small town where family was important, your neighbors were your friends, no one bothered to lock their doors, and the town closed down on Sunday to go to church. My grandparents, originally from Holland, were involved in establishing our Dutch community that still has two large windmills downtown and a population of over 13,000 today. My Dad was in the first graduating class of Lynden Christian High School in 1949, and took over his father's dairy farm. My family, consisting of two older brothers and one younger sister, was raised there. I have many fond memories of growing up on the farm: playing with kittens my sister and I would find under the barn, feeding the newborn calves, and driving the hay tractor in the summer time. Like most of my friends, my first job was picking strawberries at one of the local berry farms.

My parents, from the time I was small, taught us strong values and provided a wonderful example of what it means to have a strong and healthy family. They have celebrated over 60 years of marriage. We get together regularly for a family reunion, and that summer we spent a wonderful week with my parents, siblings and all our family members – over 40 of us now. During one of the evenings together, we honored my parents for the great example they provided to us. My dad commented that he felt he really hadn't done anything extraordinary. We disagreed. The life he thought was ordinary was, in fact, one of great example: one of integrity; one of a love for God and our family; and one of a strong work ethic which taught all of us that we are not simply handed success – that we must be committed, work hard, and do our best with the gifts we have been given. They also demonstrated a fine example of giving back. From the time I was a little girl, I remember my dad putting a quarter in my hand every Sunday for the offering at church. My parents gave generously of their money and their time in various volunteer activities.

As I became an adult, I needed to make my own decisions for how I would lead my life. I was fortunate to have such a great example in my home growing up that I adopted many of my parent's values, along with adding others that were especially important to me.

Unfortunately, many a childhood is not golden. When this is the case we can learn from the examples of things we don't want in our life. A dear friend of mine was raised in a dysfunctional home with a dad who was an alcoholic and absentee parent – obviously not a good influence. When he grew up my friend made the courageous choice to take a different path, breaking the cycle of addiction and abandonment, and is now a deeply devoted husband and father.

Your Values are Your Foundation

It is critical to identify your values as they become the foundation you can build upon to design the life you want. When you are confident in the values that will lead you, it becomes much easier to determine your purpose, and what will provide true satisfaction both professionally and personally.

As mentioned in chapter three, it is important to recognize that often people are living for someone else's values – perhaps those of a parent, a significant other, or their boss. Remember the number one regret listed in the previous chapter, "I wish I'd had the courage to live a life true to myself, not the life others expected of me." Ask yourself if you are tied up in the "have-tos" that are the success lie: working toward something you think you should be doing versus living within your own gifts and passions and striving to be the best version of yourself. If you find you are discontent and unsatisfied with your life, it may very well be that you are caught up in living in a way that is not congruent with your own values.

To quote from Palmer again, "For a long time, the "oughts" had been the driving force in my life-and when I failed to live up to those oughts, I saw myself as a weak and faithless person. I never stopped to ask, "How does such-and-such fit my God-given nature?" or "Is such-and-such truly my gift and call?" As a result, important parts of the life I was living were not mine to live and thus were doomed to fail. Vocation does not come from a voice "out there" calling me to become something I am not. It comes from a voice "in here" calling me to be the person I was born to be, to fulfill the original selfhood given me at birth by God."[18]

So how do you identify your own values? The following are a couple of exercises to assist you:

Joy Moments Reflection

One exercise I have used is a Joy Moments Reflection. Think back over the last year and remember the times that have brought you absolute joy and/or deep satisfaction, personally or professionally. What were you doing in that moment? When you complete this task, you will likely notice patterns. Family First is one of my values, and in my list I noticed repeatedly my times of delight and deep satisfaction were when I was spending time with my family.

Core Values Assessment

A Core Values Assessment will help you define what is most important to YOU in designing a life of significance. I have included a simple exercise for you in the challenge section of this chapter. As you go through the list, start by underlining every word that speaks to you. Don't give the list too much thought at first, simply underline every word where you pause and think – "Yes, this is something important to me." Remember not to choose based on what you've been conditioned to believe is a good value, but what is truly important to you. Don't worry; there are no right or wrong answers and no specific number of words you need to underline in this first go around.

Next, go back to the words you underlined, and narrow the list down to the five values that are most important to you.

Finally, prioritize the list of five down to three core values. If you find this difficult, simply compare the values against each other to determine what value trumps the other in an actual situation.

For an in-depth core values assessment with over 300 core values to choose from, go to TheSuccessLie.com.

Core Values for Your Business

It is also a worthwhile practice to set up core values for your business. Our work should be where our passion meets our purpose for being on this planet. Our work should be a place where we are fulfilled, and where we make a difference in the lives of others. If your work is not in line with your values and beliefs, it will be difficult. Having separate priorities for business and home life can become an energy vacuum and remove passion in your life.

> Our work should be a place where we are fulfilled, and where we make a difference in the lives of others.

Business values should expand to the ideals you hold personally but also what is expected from a product or service side of things. This will also allow for all team members to clearly understand what are held as priorities in the business. It can be a way to introduce new initiatives and integrate new employees quickly.

At our company, these values morphed into *The MSNW Way*, which is a list of our core values in action. Questions around these attributes are used when hiring to ensure we are attracting those who are aligned with the company culture. When there are client or employee issues, these values will provide direction. In times of decision, they provide the anchor that keeps us firmly in line with who we want to be as a company.

When Values are not Aligned

As you read this chapter and go through the exercises, you may find that your values are not aligned with your business or the work that you do. Sometimes there are situations where you are not in control of the company values. There may be others in leadership, on a board of directors, or stockholders who are setting the direction of the company. I am compelled to pause a moment to talk with readers who find themselves in this situation.

If you find yourself in a place where you are unsatisfied, or maybe even dreading to go to work, it may be an issue of personal and professional values not being aligned. Here are a few questions to ask yourself:

1. Are you excited and on board with the vision and values of your company? If so, you will feel aligned with and support the company direction. If not, you will find yourself often uneasy, and company decisions will make you uncomfortable.

2. Do you have a positive connection and shared values with the people you work closest with? If so, you will look forward to seeing them each day, and collaborating will be natural. If not, you will likely avoid them, and detour opportunities to work together.

3. Are you using your top strengths at work? If you are working the majority of time at what you like doing and are best at, you will likely be happy in your work. On the other hand, if you spend most of your day doing tasks that you find grueling or unappealing it will lead to job dissatisfaction.

As we spend the majority of our lives in a career, shouldn't our work be a place where we can do something we love?

As we spend the majority of our lives in a career, shouldn't our work be a place where we can do something we love? According to a recent poll from Gallup, only 31.5 percent of workers in the U.S. are engaged – meaning they are enthusiastic, involved in, and committed to their work; 52 percent are not engaged; 16.5 percent are actively disengaged. Which group do you fall into today?

If you do not love what you do, do something else. Make sure your work is congruent with your beliefs and you will be blessed with a career full of happiness.

Unengaged Worker Pie Chart

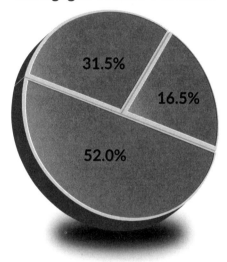

In the book *To Bless the Space Between Us,* John O'Donohue wrote a beautiful prayer on what our work should aspire to.

FOR WORK

"May the light of your soul bless your work
with love and warmth of heart.
May you see in what you do the beauty of your soul.
May the sacredness of your work
bring light and renewal
to those who work with you and to those
who see and receive your work.
May your work never exhaust you.
May it release wellsprings of refreshment,
inspiration, and excitement.
May you never become lost in bland absences.
May the day never burden.
May dawn find hope in your heart,
approaching your new day with dreams,
possibilities, and promises.
May evening find you gracious and fulfilled.
May you go into the night blessed,
sheltered, and protected.
May your soul calm, console, and renew you." [19]

When we move headlong into the daily routines of our lives, we do not always spend enough time thinking about what is important to us and why. Our priorities get left in the dust as other urgencies take over. That is why I encourage everyone to reflect on their values. It starts with knowing where you acquired your belief system and how it was created. Usually it is a combination of important people and situations that provide the impetus for the choices we make regarding priorities. Too often we approach our work, families and personal lives without considering the overall impact it will have on the values we have or what we want to achieve. Take the time to define your values. Then make the choice to live your life with the intent to set your priorities and accomplish goals in alignment with your values.

JOY MOMENTS

Take time to reflect on times in your life that have brought you absolute joy and/or deep satisfaction, personally or professionally. Write down what you were doing in that moment. Keep going until you have a list of at least 25 items. When you complete this list, you will likely notice patterns. These activities will likely correspond directly with your values – what is most important to you.

Daily Priorities Action List. An exercise that has helped me to remain focused on what is *important* versus *urgent* is as follows:

1. Determine the most important things you need to be working on in your business.

2. Prioritize what is most important for you to accomplish this week.

3. List 1-3 critical action items that you will complete today and place this list where it can be easily seen throughout the day.

4. When interrupted with an urgent request, compare it with the items on your action list, and determine what needs to be accomplished first – the new item or the items already listed. If you find the new item is more important than what you have slated for your day, put it first. However, most of the time you will probably find the "urgent" request really isn't so urgent and can be completed later.

5. At the end of the day, celebrate the accomplishment of completing your list.

CORE VALUES

Your Values are your Foundation. It is critical to identify your values as they become the foundation you can build upon to design the life you want. When you are confident in the values that will lead you it becomes much easier to determine your purpose, and what gives you true satisfaction both professionally and personally.

Using the example below as a guide, underline ten core values that are most important to you. Then, review your choices and prioritize the list to three to five core values.

For an in-depth values assessment, go to
TheSuccessLie.com

Values

Achievement	Fame	Justice
Authenticity	Family	Kindness
Beauty	Freedom	Love
Care	Friendship	Patience
Caution	Fun	Peace
Commitment	Giving	Respect
Community	Gratitude	Security
Compassion	Growth	Significance
Competence	Happiness	Strength
Competition	Health	Structure
Confidence	Honesty	Success
Courage	Humor	Truth
Creativity	Impact	Warmth
Discipline	Independence	Wealth
Education	Influence	Winning
Energy	Integrity	Wisdom
Excellence	Intelligence	
Faith	Joy	

Chapter 6

BITTER OR BETTER

---

*"Choosing the right perspective allows you
to embrace every day, overcome obstacles,
and makes the journey extraordinary."*

It was the Monday of a typical work week, the fast-paced blur where you look at the clock and can't believe the work day is over already and you need to get home. I didn't know then it would become a pivotal day, one now forever ingrained in my memory. Arriving at my house I found my two youngest daughters, four and seven years old at the time, home alone. They had been left in the care of their father for the day. When I asked where he was they said, "Daddy isn't here. He left with a suitcase."

My husband was gone. Without any notice, without any warning, he had abandoned his family. Though he had been in and out of our lives constantly with the various cycles of addiction, there was finality to it this time. He had left his own "Dear John" note on the counter to me stating he was not coming back.

The stillness of the house matched my heart as I felt frozen in time, not wanting to face the reality that what I had dreaded for years had actually happened. It was surreal – to think my husband and I had just taken a walk together the night before talking about the upcoming week, the kids' activities, and our plans for the next family vacation.

With mechanical precision, I moved through the familiar evening routine of making dinner, cleaning up, checking the next day's schedule, and getting the girls ready for bed. With baths done and teeth brushed, my daughters were in their matching fluffy robes – white with pink and blue bears. I can still smell the baby shampoo in their hair. How little they were, so precious – my everything. Then my 7-year-old asked me, "Mommy, when is Daddy coming home?" Looking at the concern in their eyes and the million questions on their faces, I simply knew I couldn't lie to them too. I got down on my knees in front of them and took them in my arms to tell them the truth. Daddy had left, and I didn't think he would be coming back.

This began the closing chapter of what had been a long and excruciating journey of 20 years. As I look back, what was going on behind the scenes was so difficult, so devastating, and so demoralizing, it is surprising that I got through it. I don't want to trivialize other's challenges with my despondent story, but instead provide a window into my pain that may help you to find some perspective on yours.

My first husband and I met as teenagers. He was a confident and talented player on the varsity basketball team. I was an energetic cheerleader. After getting to know each other on the bus rides home from the games, it didn't take long before we became high school sweethearts. Soon we were inseparable. He was the love of my life, and we married the summer after my high school graduation.

Unfortunately, my husband struggled from the time he was in junior high with the demon of drug addiction. What I naively thought was something he would surely stop when we "grew up," became the source of a great deal of pain. I began to learn all too well the vicious cycle of addiction, and what it felt like to ride the crazy rollercoaster of highs and lows. When times were good he was a caring husband and adoring father to our three daughters. When times were bad he would be distant and angry and disappear for days or weeks at a time. After a while he would come back, deeply apologetic, and agreeing to get clean and sober. We would start counseling and treatment and once again life would be good. As this pattern went on, I found myself constantly anxious, not being sure what person I would wake up to, or would come home to after work. We needed to do whatever was necessary to not upset Dad. I felt like I was walking on eggshells, making sure I was doing everything possible to keep the house happy and the kids quiet. This didn't always work as there were times when my oldest daughter would simply get fed up and tell him so, and sometimes I did too. This, of course, never ended well.

At the time it felt completely normal – this was "my normal" and something about it, however ugly, felt comfortable. And of course, I couldn't imagine giving up – as that is something I seem incapable of. Afterwards, my friends and family said to me, "How did you stay so long? How did you even survive?"

It got to a point where my husband could no longer keep a job. Willing to do anything to help him, I agreed to work full-time so he could focus solely on his sobriety. The bread-winner, the parent, and the responsible one, I played the role well of having everything together. It seemed this was always expected of me. I was the rock, the protector and defender of my family. I went to work every day, and other than the few close friends I confided in, no one knew what was going on in my life.

It is interesting what stigmas surround addiction and mental illness. When you have a spouse that has an illness like cancer, you share it freely and everyone comes around you for support. However, alcoholism, addiction and mental illness just don't make the list. They are the shameful things you don't talk about, and I protected our secret with everything I had.

Around the same time a close cousin that I grew up with was recovering from the loss of her husband after a long and painful battle with cancer. We corresponded now and then. I had reached out to let her know I was thinking of her and the kids as they grieved, and what she said back to me one day rang so true. She said, "Janelle, I appreciate your kindness. It means so much to me. But what you are going through is equally, if not more, devastating. Jim left me, and we are all mourning his loss. But the difference is, he didn't *choose* to leave. Abandonment, in many ways, is worse than death because they made the choice to leave. Everyone else who loves them has to live with that choice."

Living in the aftermath, the next few years were difficult. My oldest daughter found her escape at college and I was glad she had a new environment and path to focus on. Meanwhile, my two youngest battled every day. One was withdrawn and quiet, the other angry and extremely anxious. Both struggled with deep grief and confusion, and there were many nights they cried themselves to sleep. I kept telling them we would be ok. It was hard, but in time we would feel better. We had each other and would get through it together.

Some days it felt impossible to go on, and more than anything, I wanted to crawl into a ball in the corner of my bedroom and never get up. I had a choice to make. I could let the situation completely derail me, or choose a different perspective. So, I got up every day, put one foot in front of the other and just kept going. I relate to the quote by Martin Luther King Jr., "If you can't fly, run. If you can't run, walk. If you can't walk, crawl. But keep moving." Move I did, and my mantra became "for my girls." I even changed my computer password to this, so I would type it in as a reminder to myself every day. I made the decision to be optimistic and grateful for my family and friends who supported me, a successful business that sustained and challenged me, and my beautiful children who needed me.

I had a choice to make. I could let the situation completely derail me, or choose a different perspective.

The Power of Optimism

Whether we are naturally positive and optimistic, or we tend to spend more time on the dark side of pessimism, we will all be faced with difficult times and situations that will shake us. Also, as leaders in our organizations, everyone is watching our example, whether an optimistic perspective or one of negativity. Either one will flow down to the organization so how we "show up" is vitally important. In the book *The Power of Full Engagement*, authors Jim Loehr and Tony Schwartz say, "Energy is highly infectious, and negativity feeds on itself. Leaders have a disproportionate impact on the energy of others."[17] Our negative emotions are highly contagious. In the past, when I allowed fear or anger to show up in myself at home, it mirrored negative behavior in my children. Similarly, negative emotions shown at work would undermine my team's ability to perform at their best.

After my own challenges, life went on, for me and the kids. It was not our choice to be on our own, but it was our choice how we would respond. My youngest daughter shared her perspective on the events of her young life in her Senior High School speech.

"My father's absence created a dark place for my left-behind family. We were all sad, confused, and devastated because of his absence, and his choice to put his addiction for drugs over his love for us. However, through this painful time, my mom kept singing and speaking sunshine. Not only did she succeed in her career, but she never stopped being the mom that my sisters and I needed. She played the role of mom and dad as a single parent. She loved us unconditionally and never stopped telling us "Mind over Matter"; that no matter the circumstance we were enduring, we can create our own sunshine by choosing optimism. I would not wish to go through this grey sky again, but I have come to realize facing this specific challenge is what gave me one of my top strengths, positivity."

Malcolm Gladwell, in his best-selling book *David and Goliath*, further explains this concept of mind over matter, and overcoming difficult situations. Gladwell discloses how children who endure painful situations, specifically the loss of a father or mother, frequently come out to be the most successful, driven adults. He states, "Losing a parent is not like having your house bombed. It's worse. It's not over in one terrible moment, and the injuries do not heal as quickly as a bruise or a wound. But what happens to children whose worst fear is realized – and then they discover that they are still standing?"[21]. What happens to these children is that they go through the darkest valleys and come to discover that since they're still alive, the valleys weren't so dark after all. It builds a cumulative amount of courage and self-confidence, and gives the child strength to face the good, bad, and ugly parts of life with a smile.

As I mentioned earlier in the book, I attribute much of the success I have had to the power of optimism in my life. Trouble is simply part of our lives here on earth and this "cup half full" mentality will allow you to embrace the good things. It is a mindset that changes your outlook, your actions and ultimately your results.

> Optimism is a mindset that
> changes your outlook, your actions
> and ultimately your results.

Bitter or Better

Another example of choosing the right perspective came from a colleague of mine. He and I were discussing the challenges we had both faced in life, and he shared the challenging circumstances and painful memories of his childhood in the home of an alcoholic parent. What was interesting was that he and his siblings had all lived in the same household and faced a similar childhood experience, yet only he made the choice to allow the pain to not be wasted, to commit to life-changing decisions to propel him to a new life and to break the cycle of dysfunction that is so commonly passed from generation to generation.

You are likely familiar with the quote by Friedrich Nietzsche, the German philosopher, who famously said: "That which does not kill us makes us stronger."[22] In *Psychology Today*, Dr. Noam Shpancer comments that this notion found life beyond Nietzsche's – which is ironic, his life having been rather short and miserable – and it continues to resonate within American culture. [23] One reason is that suffering is an inevitable part of life. But the bulk of psychological research on the topic shows that, as a rule, if you are stronger after hardship, it is probably in spite of, not because of the hardship.

Our early influences can leave behind deep marks – both good and bad, that we tend to carry around for the rest of our lives. Times of hardship and trouble can make us "bitter or better." We can allow circumstances to make us frustrated and bitter, or we can make the choice to use what we have learned to develop our character and to have better, brighter futures.

Choose to Live Gratefully

You can find perspective by taking time to be grateful. Remember learning the song as a child, "Count your blessings, name them one by one?" If you are like me, you will now be humming this song and will have it in your head for the rest of the day.

My daughter had the opportunity a few summers ago to serve in a local orphanage in Guatemala and came back with an entirely new outlook on her own life and the world. Children who have been sheltered may not understand how good we have it here in the United States, however, as adults we have no excuse. Even so, don't we still find ourselves complaining at time about things that are insignificant?

Take a review of the last 24 hours. How often did you speak with an attitude of complaint versus an attitude of gratitude? Were you looking back with regret or forward with eager anticipation for positive things in your future? Let's face it, we are human and can be prone to be negative, so it is important to check ourselves from time to time and self-correct as needed.

Consider this:

> "If you have food in your fridge, clothes on your back, a roof over your head and a place to sleep you are richer than 75% of the world. If you have money in the bank, your wallet, and some spare change you are among the top 8% of the world's wealthy. If you woke up this morning with more health than illness you are more blessed than the million people who will not survive this week. If you have never experienced the danger of battle, the agony of imprisonment or torture, or the horrible pangs of starvation you are luckier than 500 million people alive and suffering. If you can read this message you are more fortunate than 3 billion people in the world who cannot read it at all." **Author unknown**

Choose to live gratefully. It requires active practice each day to focus on your blessings instead of your troubles. This is not always easy in this difficult world we live in. When things don't always go your way, evaluate and take action where possible, and let go of what you can't control. Trust that everything will work together for good.

You will face challenges. Be optimistic and do not allow negativity to take up space in your life. Even though you can't control the conditions around you, you can control yourself, your attitude and your response. We can choose a perspective that leads us forward in the life of significance we are creating, versus one that holds us back. Whether the day will be a good day, the month a good month, or the year a good year, is a matter of choosing the right perspective.

Even though you can't control the conditions around you, you can control yourself, your attitude and your response.

DEFINING MOMENTS

Take some time to reflect on the defining moments of your life and answer the following questions:

1. What significant challenges have you faced and how have they shaped the person you are today?

2. What lessons did you learn through these experiences?

3. If you could go back and do it over, would there be anything you would do differently in response to a particular situation?

Challenge Exercise

GRATEFULNESS JOURNAL

Consider keeping a Gratefulness Journal. Each day as part of my morning routine I write down three things I am grateful for. Try to be specific and write down different things every day. Doing this puts you in a positive mindset and is a wonderful way to start the day.

GRATEFULNESS EXERCISE

Taking the time to write down what you are thankful for can transform your well-being. Next time you find yourself having a negative perspective, stop and write down 10 things you are grateful for. It is impossible for our brain to focus on something positive and negative at the same time so this exercise forces our perspective to change.

Today I am grateful for:

1.   6.

2.   7.

3.   8.

4.   9.

5.   10.

TRANSFORM YOUR CAREER

SECTION TWO

Chapter 7

GOAL SETTING SUCCESS

---

*"Live intentionally, and watch your
dreams become the life you are living."*

Las Vegas is a fun venue for an industry conference, and I always enjoy a few days away from work with colleagues and friends to network and learn something new. (If you are like me, two to three days in the "night is day" atmosphere of this vibrant city is all I can handle.) One particular visit was especially good timing as business had been overwhelming and I was ready for a break.

The venue, as always, did not disappoint. At these meetings, the suppliers go all out to show appreciation to their clients, and our first evening we enjoyed a spectacular networking event under the Eiffel Tower at the Paris Hotel. The weather was idyllic – pleasantly warm with a clear sky and we had the perfect view from the outdoor vantage point of the beautiful Bellagio fountain show. I don't think any of us will forget our exotic servers who were "living tables."

This was one of many fun events where my colleagues and I had the chance to unwind and catch up. It is always nice to remind ourselves we are not alone in this entrepreneurial pursuit. We shared stories of exciting wins at work and commiserated on shared challenges we were facing in our businesses.

The conference itself was equally gratifying with an exciting line up of speakers. Even though I was enjoying myself and learning some new takeaways, I noticed my mind continuing to wander to the overwhelming list of responsibilities I had left behind at home and the office. On the first morning of the conference, the meeting room in Las Vegas was packed, the speaker engaging, and the topic interesting, yet I found myself distracted.

Though I very much wanted to be present, I was thinking about my daughter and having guilt over her basketball game I would be missing that night. Then, as if reading my mind, my cell phone began going off with texts from my daughter, who needed me urgently. I am sure there are parents reading this who can relate to the repeated pings of "Mom, Mom, MOM…. What are you doing? Why are you not answering your phone?" After quietly excusing myself to coach her through one of those "my life is over" situations typical of the average teenager, I was able to resume the meeting.

Sometimes, when my kids were younger, no matter what I was doing, I felt I should be doing something else. When I was traveling for work, I was missing my daughter's basketball game. When I was at her game, I was tempted to check my phone to see what was going on at work. It didn't matter that the game was at 7 p.m., because that is when most of our teams were working.

Over the years as my services company grew, it was often challenging to keep a balance between work and home. The building services industry goes 24/7 and it is hard to stay on top of everything. Entrepreneurs and business professionals often struggle with juggling too many balls and find themselves frustrated and overwhelmed, trying to keep up in this fast-paced world we live in. My experience was no different.

Entrepreneurs and business professionals often struggle with juggling too many balls and find themselves frustrated and overwhelmed.

I have learned some lessons along the way in growing my business. In this section, I would like to share some success tools with you that have helped me be more productive and to create more space in my life for the things that are of highest value.

We all have the same 24 hours in each day. It is up to us to use them wisely.

In working with business leaders across multiple industries, it seems everyone struggles with finding enough time. We all have the same 24 hours in each day. It is up to us to use them wisely. This begins with knowing our priorities, as we discussed in Chapter 5, and then being intentional with our time. I have found the following key performance habits provide the best process for success.

Start with a Year End Reflection

Each year the fourth quarter, and especially the month of December, is a time of reflection and planning for me. I schedule out large blocks on my calendar where I can have quiet, uninterrupted time to reflect. Though I change up the process a little bit every year to keep it fresh, the concept is the same – to take time to thoughtfully reflect on the past year to see if I have lived my values and accomplished the goals I set out for myself. What worked for me? What didn't? What have I accomplished? What am I proud of?

What am I disappointed in? What activities and experiences brought me joy and fulfilment, and which ones kept me up at night?

I like to use my journal, though any notepad will do – somewhere you can "brain dump" your thoughts on paper. I start with asking myself the question, "What did I achieve that brought me joy this last year?" With an open mind and blank sheet, I begin to write down all the significant positive achievements and experiences that I can think of. These are the events that brought a smile to my face and lifted me up – those special times that when you think of them, they make you smile all over again. Once you have completed this task, go back and look for themes. These are the type of activities you want to continue in your life, and to be mindful of as you create your plan for the New Year.

Similarly, on another blank sheet, make a list of the stressors of the previous year. Ask yourself what circumstances happened, or events were you a part of, that caused you pain or extreme stress. Think of your sleepless nights – as leaders in our businesses and families, the way to identify what is *not* working is to go to the thoughts that wake you in the middle of the night. As you put this list together and begin to look back at what has been bothering you, you will find that some things were out of your control to prevent, while many others are areas or activities that you can and should eliminate going forward. As we have talked about already, the first step to positive change in your life is to be aware of and recognize what needs to change.

Remember the seven main areas of life that we discussed in Chapter 3. This is an effective template to use to evaluate each area of your life to ensure you are living your best life – one aligned in your values and purpose. Use your journal or the worksheet at the end of the chapter to take notes. Let's go through each of these in some detail:

1. Physical – Your Health

This area of your life focuses on your health and well-being. How does your body feel today? How does your health and energy compare to one year ago – have you moved forward or back?

When I evaluate my health, I like to review the following three areas:

- **Nutrition.** Am I giving my body the right nutrition? Proper nutrition is our foundation for good health. We are what we eat – quite literally. What we put in our bodies will either fuel us properly and give us daily energy and stamina to accomplish our tasks or deplete us. Eating in an unhealthy manner will drain us of energy and we will find ourselves hitting walls. Review your eating habits over the last year and consider what changes you need to make going forward.

- **Exercise.** Am I keeping up with a consistent exercise routine? Having strong cardiovascular health and muscle strength is paramount to a healthy life. Along with nutrition, exercise also increases our energy levels as well as reduces the risk of chronic disease. Review your exercise habits over the last year to assess what is working and what you need to change. If this is an area that is difficult for you, consider asking a friend to be a workout buddy or hiring a personal trainer to hold you accountable.

- **Sleep.** Am I getting the appropriate amount of sleep that my body needs? Getting enough quality sleep is key to a healthy lifestyle. This is an area I have had to work hard to maintain. I have found that when I get a good night's sleep it makes everything in my day go better. Review your sleep habits over the last year to see if you are getting proper rest, and if not, make a plan for change.

2. Mental – Your Mind, Personal Growth

The best leaders are deeply dedicated to continuous improvement and life-long learning. They are constantly seeking ways to grow and improve themselves. With an insatiable curiosity, they constantly learn and hone their own skills.

As you look back over the last year, consider what steps you have taken to improve yourself personally or professionally. These can include items such as attending a class to learn a new skill, attending a conference, or engaging in a book study. You should be able to name specific things that contributed to your growth. Take the time to write these down now.

Another area to consider is our mind state. How is your mental well-being? As you think back over the past year, rate yourself on a scale of 1 to 10 (1 being worst, 10 being best) on whether your state of mind was more often negative or positive. What about right now? How would you describe your state of mind? What about generally? Consider whether you find yourself highly agitated and stressed, with a pessimistic outlook, or happy and fairly calm most of the time, with an optimistic outlook, despite circumstances. Some struggle more than others with this, and all of us will find ourselves somewhere on the spectrum of a mind at peace versus one that is highly agitated and anxious.

Later in the book I will talk about the power of our brain and our ability to train it to help us function better. In the meantime, use the mind-state rating to determine if this is an area you would like to improve in the coming year.

3. Spiritual – Your Values

One of the most important things to keep us grounded in our lives is the spiritual component and the alignment of our values. In Chapter 4 you identified your "why" by asking questions like, "What is important to me?" and "What is the meaning and purpose of my life?" You identified your own values, and this should be your compass.

Once you understand your role in this world it is critical to stay true to yourself and your values by ensuring you are regularly checking in on them, as well as engaging in consistent activities to keep this bucket filled. For myself, alone time on a regular basis, for reflection and prayer, restores me. I also find spending time in church singing praise songs and hearing an inspirational message both grounds and rejuvenates me for the week ahead. This is highly personal and what you need in this area will be different than what I need.

As you review the last year, consider whether you have been living according to your values and what you have been doing to stay aligned with them. Have you established regular habits and routines to keep these at the forefront? Can you identify a particular situation where you were asked to participate in a project or event that didn't align with your values? If so, what was your response to this and how can it be a learning experience for you to reinforce what is important? Using the tools at the end of this chapter, take time to evaluate the last year through the lens of your values and see whether you are on track or need to make some adjustments.

4. Family & Friends – Your Relationships

Having strong relationships that are meaningful and growing are key to a fulfilling life. We often don't pay a lot of attention to our relationships and can take them for granted – especially family members and close friends. The end of the year is a great time to review this critical life area. Did you make the time this last year to invest in the most important relationships of your life?

This would be a good time to review the exercise from Chapter 3 where you identified the people in your life that were of highest value to you and wanted to spend the most time with. Bring to mind those individuals in your inner circle and describe what the relationship with them looks like to you – specifically, your relationship with a spouse or partner, children or other close family members, close friends. How much time did you spend with them this year? What is the status of these relationships currently? Did you cherish and nurture these vital relationships, or do you have regrets about putting them in the back seat to other things? Take time to answer these questions and assess where you would like to make changes in the coming year.

In addition, review your top professional relationships over the last year. Evaluate where you have spent your time to enhance these relationships versus where you have fallen short. Write down two or three names of individuals that you want to get to know better going forward.

5. Career/Business – Your Professional Life

Many of us are in the height of our careers and spend a significant portion of our days at work. The average person is said to spend 90,000 hours at work over a lifetime – roughly 1/3 of our lives. Since we are spending so much time at work, the quality of our professional lives has a huge impact on the quality of our personal lives.

Ask yourself if you accomplished the career goals you set for yourself this last year. In your work, were you diligent about working on the things that mattered most and brought your company forward? Or did you get caught up in issues that took you away from your top priorities? A question I like to ask myself is: What is it only I can do? As I know that I have limited time, I must be working on the top things I do best – where I bring the most value. As I evaluate this, I often find I am doing things that someone else could be or should be doing and I realize that I need to delegate more. If you are having trouble with this concept, look at the times of the year where you found yourself not doing well with a particular goal, and spending nights and weekends catching up. This is likely an area where you would benefit in delegating an activity to another team member or considering outsourcing.

For every goal you accomplished, note how this happened and who contributed to your success. For those goals that were missed, identify the reasons why. Is it a process or a people issue? Sometimes we will be missing a process that created the barrier to the goal; other times the person we assigned to a task didn't have the training, the skill or the will. Evaluate what went well, and what needs to change. Look at where you are today compared to where you want to go in your career and identify the gap. This will help you put together a specific action plan to develop your career and business going forward.

6. Financial – Your Money

What is your current financial state? As you review this life area, evaluate where you are today and whether this is an area in which you are comfortable and have the freedom that you want. Financial freedom means many different things to different people. For me, having financial freedom means that I have taken steps to secure my future, so I can freely contribute to the causes that are important to me, and maintain a desired lifestyle without being stressed about money. For many their financial health is of concern and one of those items that makes the "stress list."

Now look at your financial state today compared to one year ago. Have you moved forward in your financial goals over the last 12 months? Or have you found yourself going backward? It is important to have a well-established, forward-looking financial plan that will lead you to a secure financial future.

A year-end review is a great time to take stock and make changes where needed for the coming year.

Most of us are not financial experts and we don't need to be. I recommend that everyone has a dedicated financial planner, estate attorney, and certified public accountant as your advisors. They will work in concert to establish a long-term plan that meets your goals and objectives. If you don't yet have the means for such a support team, start with your accountant who can help you identify your current financial situation and make recommendations.

7. Fun & Recreation – Your Hobbies

In the next chapter we will talk about the importance of rejuvenation to enhance the quality of your life. In working with many executives, I hear so often how there simply isn't time for vacation, or taking time off for rest and pleasurable activities.

As you evaluate the last year, ask yourself how you enjoyed your time outside of work. Here are some questions to help you evaluate this life area:

1. How much time did I take off from work in the last year?
2. How does the vacation time I took compare to how much I would like to take?
3. What do I do on a regular basis for fun?
4. What personal hobby did I consistently make time for?
5. What did I do for fun or recreation that I had never done before?

I hope you can name many fun times and exciting adventures you took part in. If not, I urge you to take time to fill this most important bucket. It is vital that we take care of ourselves so that we have the energy to be our best. You have heard the term "bucket list" – a number of experiences or achievements that a person hopes to accomplish during their lifetime. If you don't have one, perhaps this would be a good time to make one! It is a fun activity all on its own to create a bucket list of things you would like to do – on your own, with your significant other, or with your family members. Make a list along with a check mark or two next to items you would like to get to in the coming year.

Set Your Goals

Once I have taken the time to look back and determine the hits and misses of the last year, then I look ahead to what I want to accomplish in the next calendar year. Included at the end of this chapter is a goal setting worksheet that you can use as an additional resource to help you in this process.

Start with the end in mind by considering where you want to be on December 31 of next year. A helpful visualization is to imagine yourself one year from today celebrating your *best* year. What would that look like? Then once you know what you want to accomplish, you can establish your path to get there by setting challenging yet achievable goals.

> Imagine yourself one year from today celebrating your *best* year. What would that look like?

Goals are tricky. Most individuals recognize the importance of goal setting to attain a better life, but most, in fact approximately 80 percent of people, never set goals.

As an example, many individuals make New Year's resolutions, however around 58%, according to research from Statistic Brain Institute[24], give up on those resolutions after the first month of making them. Individuals make resolutions as they desire change. However, when it comes down to the commitment and hard work required to actually accomplish those changes, most people don't have the psychological bandwidth and consequently drop out in a matter of weeks.

Below are a few of the top resolutions of the last couple of years. Has one or more been on your list?

- Lose weight
- Stay fit and healthy
- Get organized
- Spend less, save more
- Enjoy life to the fullest
- Learn something new
- Spend more time with family

Though well intended, only 8% of people are successful in achieving their New Year's resolutions.[25] If you truly desire change in your life, here are ten success steps for becoming one of the elite in setting and achieving goals:

1. **Want it**. You need to really *want* change in an area of your life and *be willing* to do the work.

2. **Write down specific actionable goals**. I like to write a goal for each of the seven main life areas.

3. **Choose your key three**. Though I recommend setting goals in each life area, narrow these down to your top three. I have found I am best able to focus on three priorities. So, ask yourself, if you could accomplish just three things in the next year – what would they be? Put these at the forefront of all your planning for the next year. When someone asks you what your goals are you should easily be able to name these three, and to describe what you are doing to accomplish them.

4. **Identify the desired result** and be specific about *what* you want to accomplish, *why*, and by *when*. For example, the resolution that says, "I want to lose weight" will likely fail as it is not specific, or time bound. Instead say, "I will lose 20 pounds, so I can look and feel fit and healthy, by my class reunion on August 25." See the difference?

5. **Establish a timeline**. Make sure each goal has a timeline and an end date. As mentioned above, a goal needs to be specific and time bound. Set a completion date for the goal, along with how you will celebrate when you get there.

6. **Document your why**. As I mentioned before, having your "why," your reason for wanting to accomplish a particular goal, will help you when the going gets

tough – and the going *always* gets tough on the way to reaching a goal.

7. **Track it**. What gets measured gets done. Create specific steps to accomplish your goal – in other words, what needs to happen in order to have the outcome you desire. Reverse engineer so you have the goal broken down into manageable pieces; then, whatever your goal is, track the activities every day. This can be done in a journal, or there are several great apps on the market for measuring progress. Whether you are tracking exercise, meals, sales calls, or time spent with your kids, just seeing the results of your efforts will keep you moving forward.

8. **Get a partner**. Having an accountability partner is a great way to keep yourself on track with your big goals. Partner with a friend who has a similar goal, or just ask someone to check in on you once a week to see how you are doing. It is amazing how people will get something done just because they know someone will be asking. There is nothing like having a partner who can help hold your feet to the fire, especially when you want to give up.

9. **Plan for the walls**. Everything worth accomplishing comes with adversity. You will hit a wall as you work through any important change in your life. You know yourself and what trips you up, so plan ahead

and you will be prepared to push through when times get tough.

10. **Take action**. What is the first step you need to take in achieving your goal? Set up that call or make the appointment but take the first step now!

Everything worth accomplishing comes with adversity. You will hit a wall as you work through any important change in your life. You know yourself and what trips you up, so plan ahead and you will be prepared to push through when times get tough.

Though change is never easy, those that persevere can attest that it is worth it. By following these steps, you can accomplish impactful change and take your life back.

YEAR END REFLECTION

Reflect on the last year and answer the following questions:

1. If you had to describe the last year in three words what would they be?

2. What achievements are you proud of? What was your biggest accomplishment?

3. On the other hand, where did you miss the mark and experience disappointment or frustration? What was your biggest disappointment or learning?

4. What do you want to be different?

Challenge Exercise

ANNUAL GOALS

Theme for the Year: _____

Goal Categories:

- Physical – Your Health
- Mental – Your Mind, Personal Growth
- Spiritual – Your Values
- Family and Friends – Your Relationships
- Career/Business – Your Professional Life
- Financial – Your Money
- Fun and Recreation – Your Hobbies

GOAL	ACTION	DATE
1.		
2.		
3.		
4.		
5.		
6.		
7.		

Of these goals, what is the one big thing you would like to achieve this year that will also provide you great fulfillment? By accomplishing this one thing, it will really move the needle for you personally or professionally.

Chapter 8

SUCCESS HABITS

---

*"By using success habits, you can
maximize your performance. The result
is you will work less and achieve more."*

Earlier in the book we talked about automatic living and how if we are not paying attention we can develop bad habits that over time will lead us down the wrong path. On the flip side, I have discovered that we can institute success habits into our daily lives that can also become automatic. These habits, when set in motion over time, will become an automatic part of your routine, and you won't even think about them. The opposite of taking you down the wrong path, these success habits will move you forward faster in achieving your goals.

And, the great news is that these habits will save you time, because by implementing them, you will become more efficient. Time is a precious commodity, and by being intentional with setting routines that increase efficiency and productivity, you can seemingly increase the time in your day. Who wouldn't want that? Imagine yourself creating success habits in your life that suddenly free you up to do other things. It is possible for you to work less and achieve more.

In this chapter, I will teach you two success habits that I have used to maximize performance – Intentional Calendaring and Email Management.

Intentional Calendaring

One way to increase productivity and maximize your performance is through intentional calendaring.

In planning for a successful year, I look at the calendar for the entire year ahead and block out time according to my priorities. Prioritize those items you have determined are most important and calendar them first.

Look at the calendar for the entire year ahead and block out time according to your priorities.

Let me share with you the five steps to a successful calendar. Yours may look a little different depending on your own priorities:

1. Schedule personal rejuvenation time.

Start with planned time for yourself. Yes, you read that correctly – YOU first. I am not sure why so many of us feel guilty about taking time for ourselves. We are not bringing our best to anyone or anything if we are running on empty. Our helpful airline attendant tells us to put on our own oxygen masks first before helping others! But so many of us have work versus free time backwards because we are taught to take vacation time as a reward. With many company PTO (paid time off) plans, you need to work for a year before earning any vacation time. Often well-intended vacation plans are thwarted due to work priorities taking up the calendar, and there simply is no room left.

Remember the importance of rejuvenation. For us to perform at optimum level, we must take regular time for self-care, and understand it is not a selfish activity. I go deeper into the topic of self-care in Chapter 10.

2. Schedule family time and special events.

As family is a top priority for me, I schedule family vacations, reunions, weddings, and other special events in my calendar first. Fortunately, most schools provide their academic calendars a year or more in advance, allowing you to know when all of those parent meetings, choir concerts, athletic tournaments and school breaks are.

3. Schedule volunteer time.

Volunteering in my community and industry group is important to me, and I serve on multiple boards. If I haven't received the schedule of the next year's meetings by the beginning of the fourth quarter of the current year, I reach out to ask for the detailed list of events, so I can get the dates on my calendar for the year ahead.

4. Schedule personal growth time.

Next, I schedule time in the calendar for self-development. This includes items such as industry conferences and special training and education that will help me to grow personally and professionally. Several years ago, I learned an investment formula from management expert Brian Tracy who recommends setting aside a portion of your income to invest in your own development. He said, "Invest three percent of your income in yourself. Spend three percent of what you earn on personal research and development, on upgrading your skills and abilities, and on becoming better at performing the most important tasks that are required of you. If you invest 3 percent of your income back into yourself, you will never have to worry about money again."

Think of it this way, if you become a better leader in your organization, you will be better equipped to develop the leaders in your organization, and your organization will only become better.

5. Schedule your business responsibilities.

You now have a calendar with a lot of days blocked out for your personal rejuvenation, time for your family and other activities you enjoy, community involvement, and personal growth. What you have left open is the time that you can now fill with your various business responsibilities.

I have found that having fewer days for my work meetings and tasks only makes me more focused, and I am able to accomplish more in less time. Consider that when you have a vacation you are scheduled to take, you tend to get more accomplished in the week before you left than you did in the several weeks prior. Something about compressed time makes us more efficient.

Indeed, this phenomenon of compressed time is backed by a psychological concept known as Parkinson's law. This law states that "work expands to fill the time available."[26]

A research study on Parkinson's law found that workers given five minutes to accomplish a task were able to do so successfully in the allotted time, while workers given fifteen minutes to accomplish the same task expanded their duties to meet the given time limit.

Effective Email Management

Are you managing your email or is it managing you? One of the biggest time-suckers for most executives is their email.

In a team meeting we were talking about the challenge of getting bogged down in emails. One of my managers commented that he had over 2,000 emails in his inbox. Because he had not stayed on top of them, the box continued to grow until it was a monster in size. He was so overwhelmed at the monumental task it was going to be to get organized that he avoided it until his inbox couldn't take any more messages. The problem that he had was using his inbox as his task list. Because of this, when he read an email but didn't take care of it immediately and then remove it from his inbox, he would see it and touch it time and time again.

Here are some success tools you can use to get on top of your emails once and for all.

1. Clean your inbox to zero every day.

Think of your email inbox as a place the mail is collected but then reviewed one time and removed. Consider the way we collect our mail at home.

Most of us come home from work, stopping to grab the mail on our way in. As we stroll up our front walk we begin sorting through the mail. In it we may find an invitation to an event we have been waiting to receive, a package from Amazon, some routine monthly bills, the newest credit card solicitation, and of course, the usual junk mail. Once we have looked through the various mail pieces we have received, do we turn around, head back to the mail box and put the mail back inside? Of course not. Then why do this with our email inbox? Like our post office box, our email inbox should be a place to simply receive our mail. When we decide it is time to go to the inbox, we should review every email, and then remove it.

For every email I receive I do one of three things:

1. **I read it and delete it.** All of us get our fair amount of junk mail, as well as cc'd on messages that are informational and that we don't need to keep. I delete these as I read them.
2. **I read and respond to it right away.** Many of the emails received are asking for a quick bit of information or a response. If I can take care of the email in less than two minutes, I do it right then. No sense to come back to it later.

> 3. **I read and put it in a "to do" folder.** If the email is going to take me a little more time and possibly some research, I file the email in another folder based on the priority. Then I come back at a scheduled time where I take care of these projects.

I used to have an elaborate set up of email file folders for every department, client, and each team member that reported to me. I found over time that I had trouble searching for emails as I didn't remember what folder I put it in. Did I put that one in the department file or team file? The search mechanisms in our email programs are so sophisticated now that it is unnecessary to make it complicated. I now have just three primary email folders – a priority 1 box, a project box, and a "to read" box.

2. Choose a set time of day you will review your emails.

How often are you checking your email? In this digital society where it is difficult to ever unplug many are literally addicted to their smart phones, including checking their emails constantly. Whether you check your email hourly, several times a day, or fall victim to checking your email every time a new one comes in, you can increase your productivity by creating a system for your email.

The first thing you need to do is decide when you are going to check email and stick to this. Don't fall victim to checking your email throughout the day when you should be working on your most important priorities.

Set a specific time of day you will review your emails. I have gotten to a point where I review mine twice a day at off peak times of the day: once in the mid-morning after I have tackled my most important priority for the day, and once at the end of the work day.

Set a specific time of day you will review your emails. Reduce the times you are checking email and set specific times that you will adhere to.

You may not be in a job where you can check your emails only once or twice a day. However often you are checking them now, you can check them less. My challenge to you is to reduce the times you are checking email and set specific times that you will adhere to. It will dramatically change your performance.

3. Don't let your email distract from your most important priorities.

Many of us think we are really great multi-taskers when multi-tasking simply isn't possible. Instead we are switch-tasking. Our brains are not capable of doing more than one task at a time. Try this exercise to verify this point:

- First, recite the alphabet from A – J as fast as you can.
- Second, count from 1-10 as fast as you can.
- Now, put it together – A1, B2, C3, as fast as you can. Go!

Not so easy, is it? When we are trying to do two things at once we slow way down. We have to think about one, then the other, and then back to the first one.

Do you know that it takes an average of 20-25 minutes to get back on task once you have been interrupted? Imagine the hours you are wasting in a day every time you switch from one task to the other, such as checking an email while working on an important project.

Let's get real: Email is a serious distraction. We think we are going to take just a moment to search for a particular item in our emails, yet find ourselves 30 minutes later still responding to new messages that have come in. To avoid getting caught up in this, turn off anything that will pull you in. Shut off email notifications – you don't need to know that you have received a new email. Better yet close out of your email program altogether and only log in at the specified time you have set to check emails.

Developing success habits such as Intentional Calendaring and an effective Email Management process will maximize your performance and save you enormous amounts of time. Imagine being freed up several hours from your typical work week. This is possible. You have the power to make it happen.

INTENTIONAL CALENDARING

You learned in this chapter how you can organize your calendar as an effective business tool. Answer the following questions to get started:

1. Do you find your calendar overpacked and struggle to get everything done?

2. What are the top priorities that you want to make sure to have time for? List them here now.

3. What is currently getting in the way of these top priorities? Going forward, consider these your non-negotiables and schedule them first.

Chapter 9

JUST SAY NO

"No, should be one of the most important words in your vocabulary."

Isn't it funny that one of the most important words to say is also one of the hardest? One simple word: no. Yet, to say it brings up a flood of feelings – guilt, defensiveness, a fear of offending. Sometimes the feelings flash by so quickly we don't even notice what they are. We just know that we don't want to say that one little word. Yet, the ability to say "no," to set boundaries and build a structure that works for us, is one of the most important tools we can add to our arsenals to successfully create our best lives.

I didn't used to be very good at this, as I loved saying "yes." Who doesn't love saying "yes?" Who doesn't enjoy the look of gratitude, or relief, on the face of the person who has asked the favor? Besides, saying "yes" can at times almost be a matter of pride. With the high bar I have always set for myself and my "I can do it all" attitude, I really thought I could do it all. So, of course, I always said "yes."

As my business grew and gained traction, and I was out networking and involved in the community, my face – my brand–became well established. The more frequently I got involved in community activities and nonprofit organizations, the more I was recognized. Besides, those activities were fun for me and being involved was very rewarding. It wasn't only about me wanting to always say "yes." But as a result of my frequent participation, I was asked more and more to be involved in this event, serve on this board and attend that luncheon.

I loved to help, to bring value, to say "yes," and there are so many good things to be a part of. Soon I found myself helping regularly in my children's schools, serving on two community boards and on our international industry board. I was doing all of this while running and growing my service business. I really thought I could do it all, and I did for a while before realizing that it wasn't sustainable.

It was a seemingly small, yet very telling moment that finally pushed me over the edge. A friend wanted to meet for lunch. That was it. But I was so overscheduled, so jam-packed with back-to-back events during and after work that I couldn't find a time to fit her in – for two months. A dear friend who called at random looking to connect with me was going to have to be put on the back burner for two months, so I could fulfill all my other obligations. I had said "yes" to so many people I barely knew that I had to say "no" to someone I cared about and would have loved to have seen. The realization of how absurd the situation was hit me hard. The way I was living my life wasn't working. Simply put, I couldn't "do it all." Another thought occurred to me at that moment: who says I *have* to "do it all?"

High achievers are driven and want to accomplish things, and therefore, find it easy to get caught up in doing more and more. However, if we aren't careful, we will miss out on the very things that matter most to us.

High achievers are driven and want to accomplish things, and therefore, find it easy to get caught up in doing more and more.

I said "yes" *so much*. I wanted to. It felt good. It made people happy. It made me happy – for a while. That is, until I realized I had loaded my plate up so high that it was in danger of toppling over, taking me down with it.

I learned that saying "yes" to everything was not the path to true success. In fact, if I wasn't careful, it could become my undoing. Instead I needed to understand when and how to say "no."

There is only so much time in a day. As mentioned in Chapter 7, we all have the same 24 hours – it is up to us to be intentional in how we use them. Part of this intentionality came when I realized that everything you say "yes" to means saying "no" to something else. Think about that. It is so important I need to say it again.

Everything you say "yes" to means
saying "no" to something else.

What a tragedy it would be to get so caught up in saying "yes" to everything that comes along, that without knowing it you take away precious time from your most important priorities. Yet this happens so easily.

Warren Buffett has a famous quote about the importance of saying "no."

"The difference between successful people and really successful people is that really successful people say 'no' to almost everything."

Buffett, chairman and CEO of Berkshire Hathaway, is one of the wealthiest and most successful people in the world. Most impressive to me is that he is among one of the greatest philanthropists as well, having given over $30 billion to charity.

When we think of the most successful leaders in the world, we are usually thinking about all the famous things they "do." What we don't think about is all of the things they "don't do" in order to accomplish their extraordinary results. With the amount of demands on him every day, Buffet learned about the value of time and mastered the art of defining his top goals and setting boundaries around them.

Buffett's 25/5 rule emerged from a story his personal pilot, Mike Flint, told to the late Scott Dinsmore, motivational speaker and founder of *Live Your Legend*. Dinsmore shared the story with his audiences and it's taken off as an effective goal-setting technique.

According to the story, Flint was talking with Buffett about his career priorities and Buffett had him go through a three-step process. It's a technique that we all can use: List your top 25 goals; Circle your top five; and *Cross out the rest*. Most people presume that you should focus on the top five and from time to time on the remaining ones. On the contrary, Buffet suggests crossing the remaining 20 off the list altogether. Yes, eliminate them entirely. Then make your Top Five Plan and get working on them right away.[27] Similar to the goal setting process I describe in chapter 7, he believes that if one has too many priorities, they really have no priorities. Focus instead only on your top priorities, giving them all of your attention and energy.

What do you need to Stop Doing?

I had the privilege of meeting one of my favorite business authors and speakers, Jim Collins, several years ago when he delivered a keynote at a conference I attended. He spoke on principals from his *New York Times* best-selling book *Good to Great*. One of them was his recommendation to have a "stop doing list."

Collins asked, "Do you have a 'to do' list? Do you also have a 'stop doing' list? Most of us lead busy but undisciplined lives. We have ever-expanding 'to do' lists, try to build momentum by doing, doing, doing – and doing more. And it rarely works. Those who built the good-to-great companies, however, made as much use of 'stop doing' lists as 'to do' lists. They displayed a remarkable discipline to unplug all sorts of extraneous junk."[28]

I have adopted this discipline in my own life, making a point to eliminate unnecessary tasks and narrow down my "to do" list to my top priorities.

Here are the top five items I have learned to say "no" to:

1. **The opportunities that come up that I'm not completely passionate about.** When we choose to participate in something, we should be excited to be involved, not doing it out of guilt or obligation.
2. **The things that are not aligned with my core values and priorities.** To stay true to our values, our words, behavior, and actions must be in line with our beliefs.
3. **To those requests that are not in my wheelhouse.** Often, we are asked to do things that truly belong on someone else's "to do" list. Be sure to pass on those, or delegate them to a more appropriate person.
4. **To the things that drain me of energy.** Our time should be spent on activities that we enjoy and give us energy, not deplete it.
5. **To relationships that are unhealthy.** We will never be our best if we are constantly having to lift ourselves up from interactions with unsupportive or negative people. Eliminate these relationships.

If you are like me and find yourself having a hard time saying "no," listen up. To have the successful life you desire, you must be disciplined to say "no" more than you say "yes." Consider the top priorities that you identified in Chapter 4. It may be a good exercise for you to review them again, so they are clear and at the forefront of your mind. Then, going forward, evaluate each and every decision (what you are going to say "yes" or "no" to) against these priorities.

To have the successful life you desire,
you must be disciplined to say
"no" more than you say "yes."

You will find yourself faced with these decisions daily. As time and resources are limited, you will find that you will have to say "no" to most things that come up, in order to say "yes" and remain focused on what matters most to you.

We are often easily distracted by new "shiny" things, some even call it Shiny Object Syndrome (SOS). If you are prone to this, be aware. You have the power of choice. When the next shiny object comes your way, choose to do the following: Stop. Evaluate. And only say "yes," if it is something that you are passionate about, and that aligns with your priorities and goals. Otherwise say "no."

There is a polite way to say "no." We all have connections with other people with varying passions. Instead of saying "yes" to something that does not fully align with our passions, we can refer them to someone else we know who may be perfect for the project.

I am passionate about growing leaders, bringing value to business entrepreneurs and executives, and showing them how to break free to lead lives of legacy and significance. In addition, I am passionate about helping women who need help emerging from difficult situations so that they can live their best lives. These societal needs are something I can help with, and they align with my values and priorities. I should be dedicating my time and effort to these things, thereby allowing others with different passions to give to what matters to them. As an example, I have a doctor colleague who is very passionate about protecting salmon so that they can thrive in our waters. Another friend of mine spends volunteer hours keeping animals out of shelters and finding them good homes. Yet another is dedicated to a life of politics, to ensure businesses have the freedom to grow and thrive in our community.

The success lie led me to believe that I needed to say "yes" at all times, or else. This just wasn't true. Understanding when to just say "no" has been a key learning experience for me and has led to days of better balance and higher results. It still can be hard to say "no," but it is getting easier.

Not too long ago I took a call from a colleague asking me to participate in a brainstorming session for a local fundraiser.

It sounded intriguing and was something I would enjoy. Where in the past I would have automatically said "yes," this time I paused, realizing that agreeing to participate would compromise other commitments I had already made. Even though it was a great cause, someone else would need to join the session. I just couldn't take it on and fulfill all my other obligations. I graciously declined. And it was ok – saying "no" to a request didn't mean the world was going to end. I find I am more successful, productive, and enjoy life a lot more spending my time on a smaller number of commitments and really giving them my all.

EVALUATE YOUR YES

Reflect on your schedule and answer the following questions:

1. Do you like to say "yes," and have trouble saying "no?"

2. Are there things you have been saying "yes" to, that are taking precious time away from the what matters most?

3. What is it that you need to stop doing? Make your own stop doing list and begin implementing it today.

Top 25 Priorities. Try applying Warren Buffett's 25/5 technique to your life. What are the real priorities that are deserving of your time?

Challenge Exercise

JUST SAY "NO"

In order to focus on our top priorities, giving them all of our attention and energy, it is important to evaluate what we need to say "no" to. Evaluate yourself in the following areas:

What commitments have I made that I am not excited about? These may be things that are past their time, or that you committed to out of obligation.

Is there anything I am involved in that is not aligned with my core values and priorities? If so, they should be eliminated.

What things am I adding to my "to-do" list that are not in the area of my strengths? These items should be delegated.

What activities am I involved in that drain me of energy? These should be removed from my priority list.

Am I involved in any relationships that are unhealthy? These should be carefully evaluated and be repaired or eliminated.

Chapter 10

REJUVENATION – THE IMPORTANCE OF SELF-CARE

"By faithfully renewing our physical, emotional, mental and spiritual selves we will have increased energy for our work, our teams, and our families. The result is the capacity to live more highly-engaged and satisfying lives."

Recently I spoke to a group of CEOs about unplugging. The group was dissatisfied, as I find most executives are, with their work/life balance. Most of them couldn't think of one day in the last year they hadn't checked their work email. Others said they take their families on a one- or two-week vacation in the summer, but never fully unplug from work. They take their work phones or laptops on the trip with them, check in with the office and spend time on work emails every day.

We must be intentional about scheduling time for rejuvenation. It is a key discipline to master in order to perform at our best. I was reminded of the importance of this discipline at an industry conference a few years ago.

My company, MSNW, has been a member of Building Services Contractors Association International (BSCAI) for many years. Each January, the BSCAI holds a conference for CEOs somewhere warm and beautiful. Having been a long-time member, I have had the privilege of attending many of these conferences and find it a great time of year to take a respite from winter in the Northwest.

I chaired one of the events and came up with the theme of "Rejuvenate Yourself, Recharge Your Business." The marketing staff switched the words around to "Recharge Your Business" first, as it's a business-oriented conference. I disagreed. Unless we as individuals are operating at our highest optimal energy levels, we simply have no ability to "recharge" or bring new life to our work.

Consider the word rejuvenation. Webster defines it as:

> **re·ju·ve·nate,** <u>verb</u> \ri-ˈjü-və-ˌnāt\
>
> : to make (someone) feel or look young, healthy, or energetic again
> : to give new strength or energy to (something)

Couldn't we all use a little rejuvenation? Those in leadership positions often deal with high stress and pressure that can lead to exhaustion, if not well managed. How wonderful would it be to rejuvenate – to feel young and healthy again – with a new strength and energy for our businesses and our families?

Take Time for Personal Renewal

In the book *The Power of Full Engagement*, authors Jim Loehr andTony Schwartz state, "We live in a world that celebrates work and activity, ignores renewal and recovery, and fails to recognize that both are necessary for sustained high performance."[29] They suggest that when performing at our highest and best levels, we are drawing from four separate sources of energy including physical, emotional, mental and spiritual, and are disciplined in regular use and renewal of these energy sources. If we manage these resources effectively, we can build the capacity to live a productive, fully engaged life.

I have found in my own life, and in working with and observing other executives, that it is imperative to take time for regular personal renewal before we can be effective in our businesses. Perhaps as a result of personal beliefs or societal dogma we think personal renewal is only for those who deserve it – an award for an achievement. The rest of us who are undeserving wear the hours work like a badge of honor, boasting that we work 70 or 80 hours per week.

What would it look like in your life if you turned this around? What if instead of looking at time for your own personal rejuvenation as a reward for certain work accomplished, you saw this as a key ingredient to effective leadership, and the path to achieving significant improvement and results in your business?

What if instead of looking at time for your own personal rejuvenation as a reward for certain work accomplished, you saw this as a key ingredient to effective leadership.

Those in leadership positions face many forces that compete for our time and energy. It is easy to fall into the trap of overworking to the point of exhaustion, and rarely taking time for our own renewal. If you wonder whether this is you, ask yourself the following question:

Do you have enough energy to do everything you need to do and then still have enough energy for those you love at the end of the day? Or do you find that you have sunset fatigue – spending every ounce of your energy at work so that when you come home, you have absolutely nothing left? If the answer is the latter, you are not taking enough time for renewal.

As a busy executive, I have decisively and purposefully incorporated recovery time into my schedule. One of my habits at the beginning of each calendar year is to schedule blocks of time for the entire year. I may from time to time need to adjust dates, but when I take away a scheduled renewal time in my calendar I simply move it to another date versus allowing myself to delete it.

Make Rejuvenation a Habit

Another way I have found rejuvenation in my own life is through positive habits or rituals that provide a break from my work routine. My parents instilled many positive renewal rituals into my life that I practice with my own family today. Growing up we would have regularly scheduled meals together. Even my father who was incredibly busy running his own dairy farm would take a break each evening for the family meal. If there was more work to be done, he would go back out to the farm after dinner but would religiously take this time with the family. Sunday was set aside as a day of rest and my parents had strict rules for the type of activities allowed in order to provide rest and renewal for the week ahead. Though I sometimes fought those boundaries as a child, I now look back and recognize what a gift they were. We also took at least one week annually for a family vacation, and all family members participated. By continuing to follow rituals such as these, I have found it naturally creates a time of renewal that I would not sacrifice.

Taking the time for rejuvenation is key to effective leadership. We set the example for those around us. Certainly, we want to bring our best selves to work. When we are fresh and operating with peak energy, we create a positive environment for our teams where they too can flourish. We approach work with renewed vigor and creativity. Others see a renewed passion – it is electric and contagious. Imagine the ripple effects we could have on our teams when we showed up in this way. Imagine what things could be accomplished if others followed our new example – improved results, increased morale, even fun at work!

When we are fresh and operating with peak energy, we create a positive environment for our teams where they too can flourish.

Those in their autumn years don't wish they had spent more hours at work. Instead they regret that they didn't take more time with their loved ones. They regret missing out on that important event in a friend's life. They regret they didn't take that bucket list vacation.

Commit to scheduling regular time for rejuvenation. By faithfully renewing our physical, emotional, mental and spiritual selves we will have increased energy for our work, for our teams, and for our families. The result is the capacity to live more highly engaged and satisfying lives.

UNPLUG COMPLETELY

Evaluate your ability to unplug completely from work.

My challenge to you is to schedule periodic and consistent breaks from your work – real breaks. This means literally unplugging from your work for a period of time. If this sounds impossible, start with a short period of time – even just a couple of hours – and work your way up.

You will be amazed at the difference in yourself. Making this choice allows your team to step up and empowers them to perform.

Chapter 11

MAKE TODAY COUNT

"Start your day off right with an effective morning routine, and be rewarded with a positive mindset for a day of excellence."

The morning alarm goes off. I hit the snooze button a few times until I have procrastinated as long as I can afford to without being late to work. I take a quick shower, get ready, stop to make a quick latte and I am out the door. Breakfast? What's that – I certainly don't have time for it. Then before I know it I am immersed in my day with emails, business meetings, phone calls, and connections with whoever drops in for a chat. The end of the day arrives far too quickly; many days I look back and am not satisfied with what I have accomplished.

There were many years in my career where I succumbed to this frantic morning rush and daily "firefighting." When I came to the realization that my routine was not serving me well, I made a change that has increased my productivity exponentially.

In Chapter 5, we talked about setting priorities in order to stay focused and not get kidnapped by the urgent. In this chapter, I will share with you how creating effective rituals can multiply your results and transform your day.

Start your Day Off Right

How do you start your morning in a way that puts you in the best possible attitude for the day? When you want to have a day of excellence, it makes a difference to start with an effective routine. All of us have a morning routine already, whether we think we are creatures of habit or not. If you look back over the last week at what you did when you first got out of bed, you will likely see a pattern of doing the same things in a certain order every day.

All of us have a morning routine already, whether we think we are creatures of habit or not.

What does the first hour of the day look like for you? Are your first hour activities creating a great mindset? Are you relaxed yet energized through your morning routine, or do you run around at a frenzied pace to get out the door creating undue stress for yourself? Most of us sleep with our phones next to our beds, and 80% of smart phone users check their phones before brushing their teeth.[30] When you are not fully awake and the first thing you read in the morning happens to be an email from an upset client, think about what kind of tone that sets for your day.

There are many expert opinions on morning routines. It has been stated that "all successful entrepreneurs" start their day really early. I happen to disagree with this opinion. A previous job required my attendance at early morning meetings. No matter how often I got up at 5 a.m. in the morning for the 7 a.m. meeting, I found myself never fully awake and operating at my best until after 8 a.m. This is simply how I am wired. There are different opinions about exercise as well. Some state early morning is the best time to exercise, where others prefer the evening to create a separation between work and home.

Bottom line is your routine has to work for *you*. What do you need to do first thing in the morning in order to start your day off right?

It took me awhile and a few tweaks along the way to set up the routine that works for me. I now have a one-hour power block each morning. My "power hour" is divided into three 20-minute sections:

1. 20 minutes of quiet time – for me this means morning devotions and prayer time, and a short meditation. Refer to chapter 14 for some tips on effective meditation.

2. 20 minutes of reading time. I am a voracious reader and find it energizing to begin my day in growth-oriented reading. I set a timer, so I keep on track.

3. 20 minutes to plan my daily priorities. This is a critical step to make sure I am working on the things of highest value. A colleague of mine calls them green light activities. I plan my top 2-3 priorities for the day and schedule them in my calendar. I find it is important to do these high-value activities when I am at my best. For most of us this is first thing in the morning.

A question that I ask myself often is: What is it that only Janelle can do? What is the value that I'm bringing to the organization? Everybody has gifts that they bring to their own work. Name what those are, and make sure to spend at least eighty percent of your time on those high-value activities. Understand that what is a low-value activity for you will be a high-value activity for someone else. So, if there are tasks that your team members can do, give them the opportunity.

The goal is to get everyone in your company working most of the time within their "sweet spot" of abilities.

Some helpful hints:

1. Always schedule time for yourself first, before you let other people's needs and wants intervene.
2. Include an activity that motivates you for the day, such as inspirational reading or meditation, or listening to your favorite music.
3. Eat a breakfast that includes protein. A morning meal high in protein helps your brain produce dopamine, which gives you energy and makes you feel awake and alert.
4. Move your electronics away from your bedside and wait to check emails after your morning routine is complete.

Start your day off right with an effective morning routine and be rewarded with a positive mindset for a day of excellence.

End your Day Well

Similar to an effective workout cooldown where you unwind the body and heart rate to a resting pace and take the time to stretch the muscles you have used, a similar wind down period at the end of your day brings you to a place of relaxation and prepares your body for a good night's sleep.

Entrepreneurs and business professionals can pick up the bad habit of working at a crazy frenzied pace until they run out of daylight and crash into their beds.

Create an evening that allows your
body and mind the rest it needs,
and you will end your day well.

Here are a few thoughts to consider for ending your day well:

- **Create a separation between your work day and home life.** Do you really need to have your business emails open 24/7? Be willing to give up the addiction of checking your phone every 10 minutes (or 5, or 1). To prevent this behavior, I changed my settings, so my emails only populate when I open the program. *Entrepreneur* and *Shark Tank* member Lori Greiner said, in a recent talk, that she plugs in her cell phone to charge in her entry hall when she gets home from work and does not touch it again until she leaves for work the next morning.

- **Put a curfew on your work talk.** As a family business it is very difficult to separate work from home. When my husband and two daughters, who both work in the business, are over having dinner, it is hard not to catch up on our work days. As it will sometimes be necessary to talk business, we limit the discussions at the dinner table, and set a time where work talk ends.

- **Take time to wind down.** Think about what things you can do to prepare yourself for a good night of sleep. My family often takes walks after dinner. I enjoy spending time reading in the evening.

- **Give thanks.** Finally, take a few moments at the end of each day to pause and be grateful. We all have so much to be thankful for, and if we choose to take our minds off the troubles we have encountered in the day and instead focus on the good things, it calms our minds and spirits.

Create an evening that allows your body and mind the rest it needs, and you will end your day well.

Schedule Think Time

In my earlier years as an entrepreneur I was full of vision for my business and purpose and spent significant time dreaming and planning for the things my company would grow to do and be. Then as the business grew, it seemed that my work day got more and more compacted as there were more clients, more employees, more company issues that took time and energy. I was so busy working in my business, it seemed there was never time to stop.

One of the top strengths I bring to my work is vision and strategy. I learned that the only way to be successful in using that strength was to set aside regular time for it. You cannot create a vision or make a plan for where you'd like your company to be heading while in the midst of the day-to-day fires. I added the discipline of regular planning time.

Now Friday is one of my favorite mornings. I have a coffee date with someone special and look forward to it every week. The special someone is "me." I dedicate a two-hour period with me, my journal, and my planner for some quality think time. It's a blocked appointment in my calendar as "coffee with Janelle" so everyone knows I am unavailable during this time.

Blocking time in my calendar for appointments with myself has proven very valuable. Because it is a time away from the office, emails, and other distractions, it allows me to be fully present and clear-minded. I review my goals, reflect on the accomplishments of the last week, and plan and schedule my upcoming priorities. It is also a good time for me to determine what things I am working on that I shouldn't be and make a plan to delegate to someone else.

The habit of scheduling regular time to think and plan can help you stay on track and move forward in accomplishing your goals.

INTENTIONAL ROUTINES

Create intentional routines. Evaluate if your morning and evening routines are working for you. An effective morning routine will start your day off right, and an evening routine will help you to end the day well and prepare you for a night of refreshing sleep. Use the exercise included next to create your own morning routine.

Schedule think time. Do you take time to think? Spending quiet and uninterrupted time away from your business is critical. If you are not doing this on a regular basis, take time now to schedule a recurring appointment with yourself for this vital activity.

Challenge Exercise

CREATE A MORNING ROUTINE

An intentional morning ritual will set you up for a day of success. Think about what kind of morning would prepare you for your best day. What does it look like? Follow this five-step process to create an effective morning routine that works for you.

First, evaluate your current practice. Look back over the last week and write a list of what you do in the first hour of your day in the order that you do it.

1.

2.

3.

4.

5.

Do your current activities set you up for a day of success? If not, what needs to change, and what type of activities to you want to include?

Now, write down a new routine. Make a new routine that will prepare you for your most productive day. Include the things that will motivate and inspire you.

1.

2.

3.

4.

5.

TRANSFORM YOUR MIND

SECTION THREE

Chapter 12

GET OUT OF YOUR OWN WAY

"Personal development is the belief that you are worth the effort, time and energy needed to develop yourself." Denis Waitley

---

A few years ago, I had the honor of being invited to an exclusive leadership institute with 16 men and women leaders from around the nation. Before the class began we were asked to submit a bio about ourselves to the rest of the group. Reading the various bios was a great way to get to know each other a bit before our first meeting. One of the women stood out as she was highly-educated with a doctorate in her profession, had authored several publications, and had founded and grown a thriving practice. As I read her bio, I was impressed and a bit intimidated by her education and achievements, which I perceived as being much larger than mine. When I met her, she was everything in her bio and more. She was warm, delightful, and absolutely brilliant. When she spoke to the group, she was captivating and articulate, and had our rapt attention. Yet, as I got to know her better she confided in me that she struggled with a negative image of herself, and believed she was undeserving of her accomplishments. In an industry dominated by men, she felt inadequate. We had interesting conversations about this, as I looked at her and thought, wow, what an amazing individual. But she struggled to feel this way about herself with what she admitted was a crippling inner battle. It was undoubtedly holding her back.

Who do you see in the Mirror?

My brilliant colleague is not alone. How we see ourselves is directly related to how we portray ourselves to the outside world. We will either limit ourselves in what we are able to accomplish or may desire to prove what we can accomplish, but those successes do not bring peace and fulfillment. I like the picture of a small kitten who looks at its reflection in the mirror and sees a mighty lion. If we feel small with not much to offer, we won't invest in ourselves and will limit what we can accomplish. On the other hand, if we see ourselves as strong and capable, the possibilities are unlimited.

Why do so many people fail to grow and reach their potential, or accomplish many things and be unable to experience joy and satisfaction from it? I've concluded that one of the main reasons is a low self-image. When we have a low self-image, we feel poorly about ourselves, and tend to make the situation worse through negative thoughts and critical self-talk. If we don't feel worth the effort, the image we have of ourselves will remain low without the chance to improve.

Unfortunately, negative, critical self-talk can be ingrained in us from childhood. In their book, *The Answer*, John Assaraf and Murray Smith speak to the negative messages children receive growing up. "By the time you're seventeen years old, you've heard 'No, you can't,' an average of 150,000 times. You've heard 'Yes, you can,' about 5,000 times. That's 30 nos for every yes. That makes for a powerful belief of 'I can't.'"[31]

For some people it is easier to let go of this lens we view ourselves through, for others it feels like a constant battle with our inner critic. It takes time and work to change this perception that has been reinforced for years. The good news is by choosing to have positive thoughts about yourself, you can begin the process to change and improve your self-image. Here are a few ways I have found to be helpful in silencing our inner critics.

Guard Your Self-Talk

One way to build your self-image is by guarding your self-talk. If you think about it, you will realize you talk to yourself many times a day. Is that self-talk positive or negative? Are you being kind to yourself or critical? When faced with a problem do you tell yourself, "I've got this – I will figure it out" or instead say, "I've messed up again – I never get it right." It can be helpful to log your thoughts to determine how you are doing.

Take time to be kind to yourself. You can be kind to yourself with the intention of being more kind to others, but it starts with you.

Put down the negative thoughts and chatter going on in your mind. Put down the self-criticism and judgement that you are allowing in your life. You have the power to let go of these things a little more each day. Here is how:

Throughout the day, recognize when negative thoughts begin to surface. If you pay attention you will notice yourself sorting through unpleasant thoughts right before the unhealthy chatter begins. Recognizing when this happens is the first step to correcting this unconscious behavior. When it becomes conscious you have the power to do something about it.

Don't let yourself get caught up in negative thinking. Rather than giving yourself a hard time, think about how you might react if a good friend of yours came to you with similar thoughts and feelings. How would you respond to them and help them? Of course, you would respond with kindness and care. You would meet them at whatever point they were at and encourage them. Why then, is it *so* hard to apply this same kindness to yourself? In the moment when you discover yourself being unkind, approach that with kindness. Instead of getting frustrated and heaping more judgement on yourself, think instead, "I don't need to do that anymore."

When you find yourself with a negative thought, change it to a positive one. If this is difficult for you, ask someone who cares about you and knows you well to help create a list of positive, affirming words. Be ready to pull this list out when the negative thoughts creep in. Remember to stop and allow the body and mind to find a place of ease. Build a firm foundation of health and happiness in your mind. You have the choice and the power to say "no" to negative self-talk; believe in yourself and the value you bring. I will share more about a process to train your brain to gain power over your thoughts in a later chapter.

When you realize your own special value, you will see yourself as strong and capable. You will believe you are worth investing in. The result will be growth and development and living up to your full potential.

Focus on Your Strengths

Change your focus to all the things you excel at. What are your strengths and how can you choose to use them to make life better for yourself and others? Turn around the negatives and focus on your positive attributes. Anytime you struggle with feelings of inadequacy, take the time to stop, take a breath, and reassess why you are having these feelings. Often, we overlook our greatest assets, so by intentionally examining ourselves in the mirror to find our inner lions we can choose who we see.

If you need help in identifying your strengths, the challenge exercise at the end of the chapter can be helpful. There are also several others on the market. One I like is *StrengthsFinder 2.0* from Gallup, where you can learn your top five personalized strengths or talents. Gallup Education developed this assessment and introduced the first online version of *StrengthsFinder* in the best-selling book *Now, Discover Your Strengths*. If you buy the book, you receive an online assessment code to take the test. It is a simple assessment to take and explains the unique ways you experience your strengths every day and how they influence one another.

Another helpful way to identify and confirm your strengths is to use those who know you well as a resource. I found this challenge in the book, *Unique Ability* by Shannon Waller.[32] The exercise was to ask five or ten of your closest friends or colleagues, whoever you trust to be honest, to write a list of positive character qualities that come to mind when they think of you. More than just affirming words, she talks about all of us having a unique ability – something that stands out as an ability that is special and comes easily to us. I did this exercise many years ago during a transition in my life and asked a wide variety of people including family members, friends of many years, work colleagues, and my pastor, and found it to be extremely helpful. What was most interesting was that even though these individuals spent time with me in several different categories of my life, their assessment of my unique abilities was the same. It was affirming and humbling. Once you have this list of qualities and abilities from those who know you the best, it can be a great stabilizer when you find yourself stuck in self-doubt and negativity.

Positive Thoughts

Another strategy I have used for positive change is choosing my thoughts.

What was your first waking thought today? Some days we wake up ready to take charge of the day, but we have all had days where we would love to simply pull the covers back over our heads when we hear the morning alarm.

What were your main thoughts over the last 24 hours? Were they thoughts of hope, love, thankfulness, or worry, fear, and escape? Our thoughts can become our reality, so it is important we monitor our thoughts to make sure they are positive ones.

One of the negative thoughts I have had to work hard on is worry. We all know that we shouldn't worry; that worry doesn't help us; and that worrying about a situation doesn't change anything about the situation. Unfortunately, many of us tend to worry anyway; and in fact, sometimes the act of worrying can be not only disheartening but debilitating.

I had a situation earlier this year with my husband Graham, where my tendency toward worrying took a mole hill and turned it into a mountain.

Graham had gotten the newest Apple sport iWatch for his birthday. He was having fun tracking his runs and playing with the text feature. We were carpooling; he dropped me off at an appointment and let me know to text him when I wanted to be picked up. He was going to go on a short run with a friend who lived nearby. About 30 minutes before the end of my appointment I texted him to let him know when I would be ready for pick up. I didn't hear back. No problem – he is probably still running, I thought. Ten minutes before the end of the appointment I texted him again. Nothing. This was strange, as he usually got right back to me. I called his cell phone and got no answer. Little alarm bells started going off in my head. My appointment finished, and I called his cell again and this time left a message, then sat down in the reception area to wait. An hour had now gone by and the office I was at was about to close. At this point, my thoughts went from he is still running, to something must have happened to him. Maybe he was hit by a car; maybe he had a heart attack. Why didn't I ask where he was running? Should I call the hospital? I wouldn't even know where to start in trying to find him.

I called again to no avail and also texted his friend but got no reply. I called my daughter to see if she had heard from him. Then I finally called his friend's wife, who was heading home, and she said she would check to see if her husband (and mine) were there. Almost immediately, my husband called. He had been at our friend's house the entire time! He had left his phone in the car thinking that he would get a text from me on his new iWatch. What he didn't realize is that the texting feature only works when you are a short distance from your phone. I had my poor husband in a ditch or the hospital, when he was relaxing with a beer in hand. You can imagine we had a nice discussion regarding communication on our way home.

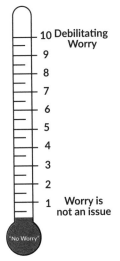

This story demonstrates how our worrying can go from zero to 90 in a heartbeat if we are not careful. How are you doing on the worry spectrum? It can be helpful to evaluate if this is a problem you need to work on. Ask yourself the following questions: Do you find yourself often with a pit in your stomach about something? Does worry wake you up in the middle of the night? Do you often hear news that could be taken several different ways, but find yourself almost immediately jumping to the worst-case scenario in your mind? Do you see problems more than opportunities? Do you find yourself dwelling on regrets of the past, or worrying about the future, versus living in the present?

I love this quote on living today from Lisa Wingate, author of *Before We Were Yours*. "Life is not unlike cinema. Each scene has its own music, and the music is created for the scene, woven to it in ways we do not understand. No matter how much we may love the melody of a bygone day or imagine the song of a future one, we must dance within the music of today, or we will always be out of step, stumbling around in something that doesn't suit the moment."[33]

Whether you scored yes to the questions on worry, or only find yourself occasionally dealing with this problem, all of us are somewhere on the worry spectrum, and can learn how to worry less. We certainly have many things in our personal and business lives that can bring us concern, but there is a difference between concern and worry:

- Concern means realizing what the problems are and calmly taking steps to address them.

- Worry means going around in maddening, futile circles, while simultaneously failing to deal with the problems.

Haven't we all been in situations that have us running in circles? When this happens, we become ineffective and can't help those who need us, like our business teams, spouses, children, or friends. More significantly, we can't help ourselves.

A favorite author, Dale Carnegie, tells us in his book, *How to Stop Worrying and Start Living*, that one of the worst features of worrying is that it destroys our ability to concentrate. When we worry, our minds jump here and there and everywhere, and we lose all power of decision. [34]

Carnegie shares a magic formula that he got from Willis H. Carrier, an engineer who launched the air-conditioning industry, and who headed the world-famous Carrier Corporation, in Syracuse, New York. After facing a potential failure, Carrier developed a formula to help solve worry situations with three steps:

"Step 1: I analyzed the situation fearlessly and honestly and figured out what was the worst that could possibly happen as a result of this failure.

Step 2: After figuring out what was the worst that could possibly happen, I reconciled myself to accepting it.

Step 3: From that time on, I calmly devoted my time and energy to improve upon the worst which I had already accepted mentally."[35]

"When we force ourselves to face the worst and accept it mentally, we then eliminate all these vague imaginings and put ourselves in a position in which we are able to concentrate on our problem."[36] Since learning this practice, I have used it often, and found it a very helpful anti-worry technique.

Another practice I have used to help me conquer worry and other negative thoughts in my own life is to listen to my body and recognize when I am allowing worry to take over. I know I am in trouble when I begin to obsess about a particular business problem or personal issue. When this happens to me, I examine what specifically it is that I am worrying about and write it down. It seems simple, but just the act of putting it on paper begins to ease the anxiety, and I can think more clearly. Once I have identified the issue, then I write down what I can do about it. Though there may be some things I cannot change, there is always some step that can be taken to move the situation in a positive direction. So, after preparing the various alternatives, I carefully make a decision on a plan of action, and immediately begin to carry it out.

When has worry changed an outcome? The act of writing down my worries and then choosing to do something about them has helped me break free from the paralyzing effect that uncontrolled worry can have.

We can have better peace of mind, not when circumstances change, but when our attitude changes. This is accomplished by making an intentional effort to choose positive thoughts, to control negativity and critical self-talk, and by eliminating worry.

Let me end this chapter with a wonderful meditation by Max Lucado from his book, *Anxious for Nothing*. It is a great reminder to choose our thoughts carefully and to make each day a great day.

> *Today, I will live today.*
>
> *Yesterday has passed.*
>
> *Tomorrow is not yet.*
>
> *I'm left with today.*
>
> *So, today, I will live today.*
>
> *Relive yesterday? No.*
>
> *I will learn from it.*
>
> *I will seek mercy from it.*
>
> *I will take joy in it.*
>
> *But I won't live in it.*
>
> *The sun has set on yesterday.*
>
> *The sun has yet to rise on tomorrow.*

Worry about the future? To what gain?

It deserves a glance, nothing more.

I can't change tomorrow until tomorrow.

Today, I will live today.

I will face today's challenges with today's strength.

I will dance today's waltz with today's music.

I will celebrate today's opportunities with today's hope.

Today.[37]

ELIMINATE WORRY

Identify if worry is not a big problem for you or if you find yourself often consumed by anxious thoughts. Ask yourself the following questions:

1. How do you rate yourself on the worry spectrum? On a scale of one to ten, one being worry is not an issue for you and ten being it is debilitating.

2. If you score high on the worry spectrum, use the exercise I described in this chapter to name a current problem you are worrying about and write it down. Describe the problem in detail and what you are worrying about.

3. List the potential outcomes.

4. Determine what the action is you can take to move forward in solving the problem. Then, take action.

Challenge Exercise

FOCUS ON YOUR STRENGTHS

Change your focus to all the things you excel at.

What are your strengths and how can you choose to use them to make life better for yourself and others? Turn around the negatives and focus on your positive attributes. Use this exercise to help you identify what your strengths are. Ask yourself the following questions:

1. Thinking about yourself in the workplace, what are you really good at? Make a list of the items that come to mind. These are your strengths.

2. What have others told you that you are good at? In what situations do you find that people come to ask you for help? See if those items match what you already wrote down or add them to the list.

3. Ask your teammates for feedback. Often our own team members will know us better than we know ourselves. Ask them for five of your personal strengths – where you bring value to the organization. Add these to your list.

MY STRENGTHS

Now look at this list and the strengths listed. Rank them in order of what you are good at, and what you love to do. This will give you a great starting point for learning or confirming what you should be spending most of your time on.

Chapter 13

CRUSHING SELF-SABOTAGE

---

*"The only thing we can control
100% of the time is ourselves."*

Bill was a top-performing manager in my company. He was what every CEO hopes for in a manager: He was bright, extremely talented, and ran his department as if he owned it himself. He had a number of certifications and years of industry experience. Our customers loved him, and his team loved him. There was one problem – he was hot-headed.

Bill walked into the office some Monday mornings and everyone fought the urge to duck under their desks. He was bristling with tension and it was obvious in every fiber of his being. We knew something was wrong – perhaps he had a negative interaction with a customer or team member.

When Bill got like this someone was sure to get the brunt of his frustration as he would lash out at everyone in his path. Bill's team loved him, as 90 percent of the time he was a wonderful boss who readily complimented his team and was the first to roll up his sleeves and work alongside them. Unfortunately, the other 10 percent was the problem, as Bill was unable to behave in a consistent way.

In over 20 years of working with exceptional leaders, I have found the biggest roadblock to one's success is the ability to manage emotions. It is the number one thing that trips people up and often brings them to a place of complete failure. They may be extremely smart, talented and skilled, but they can't manage emotions such as anger or impatience. This results in erratic behavior that they can't seem to change. The bad behavior erodes trust, taking away from their ability to build strong teams and to accomplish results.

It doesn't matter how talented you are if you have a flaw like this in your leadership skills. In Bill's case, the lack of emotional consistency over time broke trust. As his team was never sure what mood he would be in when he would show up, they began to be on guard, and tiptoe around issues to avoid setting him off. Eventually Bill moved on, as this lack of self-management derailed his leadership abilities.

If we want to live our best life, we need to find a way to break through the glass ceilings in our lives to reach the next level personally or professionally. A leadership ceiling is something that prevents us from going where we want to go.

What is in your way? What is holding you back from being everything you were called to be? What stops you from being the person that God has called you to be, or from doing the things that He has called you to do? Is there something holding you back from being the leader you want to be, the business owner, the parent, the spouse, or the friend? This will look a little different for each of us, but we all have barriers that hold us back – some self-imposed, and others caused by people and circumstances.

What is holding you back from being everything you were called to be?

Identify Your Blind Spots

There are barriers to your leadership. Some call them our blind spots. It's usually something that you don't realize is a problem – you can ask those who work for you, or those closest to you like your spouse. Some of us are very good at knowing what they are, and even work on them for a while, but they tend to keep getting in the way.

When we are not aware of these blind spots, we likely do not manage them well. If we can become aware, we can eliminate or reduce the impact of them.

The only thing we can control 100
percent of the time is ourselves.

So how do we start? The first step is to improve our self-awareness. The best chance of changing ourselves for the better is to first know ourselves. Then from our own self-awareness, comes self-management.

Personality assessments such as Birkman, DiSC, and EQ-i are very helpful in raising self-awareness. I have learned a lot about myself by taking them. We also have taken our entire management team through the assessments and found the process a great way to get to know each other, as well as to learn how to work better together.

These type of assessments provide a common language that individuals can use to better understand themselves and others. When I first took the DiSC assessment, I learned it was much more than just a personality test. It has the power to enhance productivity and communication, to help us understand our strengths and weaknesses, and how we interact in the workplace. One of my favorites is the Birkman Assessment. Like others it breaks down person-alities in quadrants but rather than just how we act it dives deeper. Birkman insights demonstrates what we like, how we appear to others, what are needs are, and how we react under stress.

The concept is simple, there are four quadrants: Doer, Communicator, Thinker and Analyzer.

1. **Doer or Dominance personalities** *place emphasis on accomplishing tasks with an eye for results.* They place focus on the bottom line of issues and tend to have more confidence in the workplace. The dominance personality sees the big picture and can be blunt when communicating with others. They are keen to accept challenges and get straight to the point of issues. Typical jobs include physician, entrepreneur, construction, IT.

2. **Communicator or Influence personalities** *place emphasis on persuading others.* They value openness in the workplace and find it to be the optimal communication strategy. These personality types have strong relationships in the workplace. They bring a wealth of enthusiasm to any group they are a part of. They are usually optimistic and love to collaborate with others. Influencer personalities appreciate being praised for their accomplishments in the workplace. Typical job types are sales, event planner, and entrepreneur.

3. **Thinker or Steadiness personalities** *place emphasis on cooperation, sincerity, dependability.* They are the ones who value routine and structure. In the workplace and at home, steadiness personalities don't like to be rushed and instead appreciate taking their time on projects and paying attention to the small details. Often, these personality types have a calm manner and approach to obstacles. Their supportive actions make them invaluable to the day-to-day mechanics of a workplace. Typical jobs include librarian, writer, counselor, and trades.

4. **Analyzer or Conscientiousness personalities** *place emphasis on quality and accuracy, expertise, competency.* They tend to be very sensitive to the small details, but their sensitivity makes them perceptive to others' nuances. They value productivity but can work very well independently, they don't need reassurance as much as they need a sense of responsibility in the workplace. Typical jobs include accountant, lab tech, banker, and attorney.

Knowing yourself in reference to the Birkman or other assessment can do a myriad of things regarding workplace performance. It can increase your self-knowledge, help you understand how you respond to conflict, and understand what motivates you and your team.

Every individual's score will be a little different. These assessments will tell you your natural state of being – how you arrived on this planet. These basic characteristics are the identifiers of who you are, and everyone will have a blend of all, but generally with one or two dominating characteristics. These scores won't change whether you are 20 years old, 30, or 50.

The EQ assessment evaluates your emotional intelligence. EQ is the ability to monitor one's own and other's emotions and to act accordingly. Unlike your IQ, your EQ is the one score you CAN change. The assessment can help you to understand what your typical behaviors and responses are and what to do to modify these to be a more effective leader. You can keep improving and moving the needle.

Get to Neutral

At the SmithBucklin Leadership Institute, led by CEO Henry Givray, I learned about an interesting concept in self-regulating called "Getting to Neutral."[38] In order to self-regulate you must first understand your current state of emotion. Even though we experience many emotions, there are essentially only three ways we can feel in any given situation.

Positive   **Neutral**   **Negative**

When something happens, it is natural to have an "automatic" response. This automatic response will be either positive, negative, or neutral, and will come from biases developed over many years based on your individual life circumstances and experiences. The name of the game is to get yourself to neutral as soon as possible. Then you can be more objective and address the situation in the most effective way.

To provide an example of this dynamic, imagine the following scenario: You are attending a regular meeting at your office where a different person comes in each month to speak on a variety of topics. Your facilitator enters the conference room to announce the guest speaker for the day, and lets everyone know this very special guest, currently waiting out in the hallway, will be doing a demonstration with a live snake. This announcement causes some immediate emotion in the participants and varies by individual. You saw snakes in a zoo as a child and feel neutral about today's presentation. Another person in the room raised snakes as a teenager so is filled with excitement and feels positive; a third person was bitten by a snake when hiking a few years before – obviously this produced a negative response. See how very different these responses are from just three individuals because of their personal experiences.

Do you know your own biases – the trigger points that will set off a positive or negative reaction? Learn them. Staying neutral is hard. Become aware (conscious). You have a choice!

> Once we become more aware
> of our own triggers we can
> begin to better self-manage.

Once we become more aware of our own triggers we can begin to better self-manage. In any given situation, get yourself to neutral.

The Desired Outcome

Another tactic for self-regulation is to take a moment before tackling something hard for you with someone and to "start with the end in mind." Think about the desired outcome and what's needed *before* you act or react.

- Your words really matter – choose them carefully. Scripting helps.

- Your action or reaction will negatively or positively affect the outcome.

- Your words and actions will tend to be magnified – especially in a position of leadership. Remember how important your body language is – 90% of communication. People can "feel" your energy. Are you calm, angry, upset?

Be Willing to Break Yourself

Sarah Robb O'Hagen, CEO of fast-growing indoor cycling company Flywheel Sports, was one of the keynotes at a recent conference I attended. A successful entrepreneur and author of the book, *Extreme You*, she was inspiring in her energetic keynote. [39] Sarah shared some of her own life challenges and failures, and how it prompted her to make necessary changes. Sarah encouraged us to "break yourself to make yourself." She helped us see that it is ok, and important, to break yourself as a leader – to think about what is not working and be willing to re-invent yourself. This resonated with me. I find it is critical step for leaders to come to grips with what is holding them back. We need to identify our blind spots and learn to self-regulate. And, we may need to break ourselves, as often we are the ones standing in our own way. Only then can we have the awareness and power to make positive change for the future.

THE EVENING CHECK-IN

At the end of the day, take just a moment to reflect on how you handled yourself throughout the day.

Ask yourself the following questions:

1. Did your interaction with others build them up or take them down? See if you can name at least three interactions where you made a positive connection.

2. Are you pleased with the communication you had with others throughout the day?

3. If not, identify what you will do differently tomorrow.

Challenge Exercise

KNOW YOUR BLIND SPOTS

We all have blind spots in our leadership. These are the personal barriers that get in the way of our effectiveness as a leader and thwart our happiness and success. These barriers will be different for each one of us, and when they "rear their head" they will hold us back from being our best, and from achieving the results we desire.

The first step to overcome these blind spots is becoming aware of them. Once you are aware of your blind spots, and understand how damaging they are, you will desire change. The second step is to make a plan of action to remove these barriers to your success.

Here are 5 common Success Barriers:

- Subconscious Mindset. A powerful belief you hold close that unconsciously effects your reactions and decision making.

- Values Conflict. The work you are doing, or the outcomes you are striving for, do not align with your core values.

- Limitation. A definitive gap or inability that you are not able to change or improve.

- Capability. A deficiency in your capabilities or current behavior, that can be improved with training and/or learning new skills.

- Weakness. A deficiency in your management style, behavior, or habits that you can change or improve.

Review the list of common success barriers. For each one, identify one to three things that currently hold you back.

For each success barrier you have listed, what has been the impact on yourself of others?

Finally, what action are you going to take to improve or eliminate this blind spot?

Chapter 14

TRAIN YOUR BRAIN

"Train your mind to be calm and you will increase your focus and productivity."

It's 8 a.m. on a Monday morning and you have settled in at your desk to prioritize your day. With your three most important tasks clearly outlined, you dive into the first project. Before you even realize it has happened, your mind has wandered away from what you were working on. You find yourself thinking about the school function you need to attend that evening for your child and that you can't forget to leave work on time. You remember that you failed to fulfill the promise you made to a co-worker to get them a report yesterday. You wonder how your mom is doing as you haven't called her yet this week. All these thoughts have just swarmed through your mind and this is just in the first few minutes of your day.

So, now I ask you: Do you have a busy mind?

As a mother, wife, and business owner, I struggle with what I like to call "Monkey Brain." My racing mind is so full of competing thoughts, feelings, and to-do lists that it is similar to a monkey jumping around from one thing to another and back again.

Research on brain science suggests that we have between 60,000 and 80,000 thoughts per day. That's an average of 2,500 to 3,000 thoughts per hour. That's incredible! These thoughts are happening automatically and at a rapid pace, yet we do have the ability to slow them down.

This is good news. You can actually get rid of the monkey! You have the ability to slow your thoughts down and process them calmly and methodically. In this chapter I will share with you how I have learned to train my mind, and how implementing meditation and other brain-enhancing exercises has helped me to enjoy true peace of mind.

Your Powerful Brain

I find it fascinating how powerful our brains are, and yet how little attention we pay to them. Our brains truly control everything about us! The exciting thing is that we can do things to help our brains function better and doing so can transform our minds.

Dr. Daniel G. Amen, in his book, *Change Your Brain, Change Your Life*, describes the brain in this way:

> "Your brain is involved in everything you do and everything you are, including how you think, how you feel, how you act, and how well you get along with other people. Your brain is the organ behind your intelligence, character, personality, and every single decision you make.

> In about 400 BC, Hippocrates wrote, "And men ought to know that from the brain, and from the brain only, arise our pleasures, joy, laughter, and jests, as well as our sorrows, pains, despondency, and tears. And by this, in a special manner, we acquire wisdom and knowledge, and see and hear, and know what is foul and what is fair, what is bad and what is good, what is sweet, and what is unsavory...And by the same organ we become mad and delirious, where fears and terrors assail us...All these things we endure from the brain, when it is not healthy...In these ways I am of the opinion that the brain exercises the greatest power in the man. This is the interpreter to us of those things which emanate from the air, when the brain happens to be in a sound state.

With a healthy brain you are happier, physically healthier (because you make better decisions), wealthier (also because you make better decisions), and more successful in everything you do."[40]

He goes on to talk about how taking care of your brain with the proper nutrition, specifically brain enhancing nutrients such as vitamins B6, B12, D, and omega-3 fatty acids, choosing positive thoughts, meditation, and spending time with happy, healthy people can actually boost your brain function. [41]

Mindfulness Matters

Mindfulness is certainly a buzz word today. With mindfulness we can learn to realize that our emotions are one small part of our experience, versus the whole experience. We can develop important insight to our emotions, thoughts and behavior. It is defined in Merriam-Webster as follows:

> ### Mindfulness
>
> 1. the quality or state of being mindful.
>
> 2. the practice of maintaining a nonjudgmental state of heightened or complete awareness of one's thoughts, emotions, or experiences on a moment-to-moment basis; also: such a state of awareness.

A few years ago, I got the opportunity to learn more about mindfulness when I met and worked with Joe Burton, the founder of the mindfulness program, Whil. Whil provides goal-based resilience training for individuals and companies to reduce stress, increase their emotional intelligence, and improve their performance. In a keynote Joe provided to our industry board of directors, he shared his own story of being a highly-stressed business owner on the edge of burnout; how he adopted mindfulness and found it to be transforming in his whole life. He then created Whil to help others better deal with stress using specific techniques through an online platform.

Stress is a huge problem in the United States. A cover story in *Time Magazine* called stress America's number one health problem back in the 80's[42], and with our continued heavy work pace as well as the progression of technology, it is getting worse. We now have four generations at one time in the work place, and three of those four generations are in the danger zone as far as stress. Stress is a modern boogeyman, keeping nearly half of us, 45%, up at night, per the American Psychological Association. [43] From their 2016 survey, *Stress in America*, researchers state, "significantly higher percentages of adults report that stress impacts their physical and mental health. For example, a substantial number of individuals report physical and mental health-related symptoms, such as headaches or feeling anxious or depressed."[44] In the graph below, adults were asked to rate their average stress level on a 10-point scale. Scoring a 1 would mean little to no stress, 10 being a great deal of stress.

Over time, the younger generations are struggling more and more with stress, with a higher percentage of all adults reporting levels of extreme stress. For all of us, the mental health symptoms of stress are growing and if the symptoms continue to grow at these rates it is predicted that by 2031, over 45% of the population will be under extreme stress. [45]

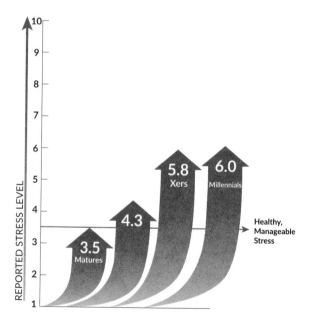

Source: *APA Stress in America: The Impact of Discrimination Report, 2016*

The "stress hormone" cortisol, when it gets out of control, can actually change the brain function to be in a constant state of fight-or-flight. Neuroscientists have discovered that chronic stress and cortisol can damage the brain.[46] As we all have only one brain for life, we can take better care of it in many ways, one being to reduce stress.

How to Incorporate Mindfulness

Incorporating mindfulness can help to ease stress and anxiety. In a 2018 study published in the journal *Psychiatry Research*, participants who learned how to effectively use mindfulness through various approaches handled stress better and had a lower hormonal and inflammatory response than those who didn't master those techniques.[47]

> Incorporating mindfulness can help to ease stress and anxiety.

As I talk to my colleagues about how they are reducing their stress, I hear more and more business leaders discovering the benefits of mindfulness or brain training in their personal and professional lives. By incorporating a practice of a simple meditation routine each morning, I have found that it has not only reduced my stress, but also helps me to be more in tune with my body. For those of you not familiar with the practice of meditation, it is simply finding time alone in a quiet spot where you can rest the mind from all of its busyness. Putting everything else aside and causing the mind to be calm and silent, even for just a few moments, can bring a state of deep peace.

Admittedly, when someone first mentioned to me that I should consider using meditation on a regular basis to combat stress, I was skeptical. Not knowing much about it, my mind immediately went to the visual of crystals and sand boxes, and monks sitting cross legged in stillness for long periods of time (that didn't sound comfortable, and frankly, I thought it a bit weird). How could that be helpful? As I got to learn more about it, I realized meditation is, in fact, so much more. It is a process by which we stop and bring a sense of calm to our bodies and brains. In doing so, this evidence-based routine has the ability to help us operate in a more present and peaceful state of mind. The concept sounded like it was worth giving it a try.

A friend of mine suggested a guided meditation app. "Headspace" was the one I started with, though there are many others on the market.

I started with the beginner series and a 10-minute guided meditation. The first few sessions didn't go well as I found it nearly impossible to sit still in silence. After one or two minutes I was opening my eyes to check the timer – *am I done yet?* Not one to give up easily, I kept going. In time, I found the minutes went faster and I was able to keep with the routine until the helpful voice of Andy Puddicombe (a former Tibetan Buddhist monk and the co-founder of

"Headspace") would let me know the session was complete. Andy would say, "How are you feeling right now?" There were times where I didn't feel any different. However, as I continued the new habit, with a bit of wonder, I began to find that more times than not, I felt better, calmer, and clearer-minded.

As mentioned, it is challenging to sit in silence, as the mind will immediately begin to wander. It was encouraging to learn this is typical for the human mind. Psychologists Matthew Killingsworth and Daniel Gilbert of Harvard University conducted research showing that our mind wanders 46.9% of the time. Says Killingsworth, "This study shows that that our mental lives are pervaded, to a remarkable degree, by the non-present." [48]

When I meditate, a helpful aid to keep my mind from wandering is to have an anchor to focus on. Think of it this way: Picture a boat that is securely anchored. It doesn't matter that the winds pick up, if a storm brews, or when the tides come and go. The boat may sway a little with these outer forces but the anchor will hold it fast. This is the same way with meditation. As you are meditating, your thoughts will come and go. This is completely normal and each time you can let them go with the focus on an anchor. For me, it is my breath, but it can be listening to sounds, or focusing on a particular word or phrase. It can be whatever works for you.

The Mind Shift

As you become more aware of your thoughts and emotions, you will likely find times when negative thoughts pierce your mind, whether or not you want them to. Before you know it, you begin to obsess on the negative thought. These can be thoughts of judgement or lack of generosity and kindness toward yourself or others. If you allow those thoughts to control you, they will have consequences.

In Chapter 12 I talked about how low self-image, critical self-talk and negative thoughts can impact our peace of mind. You may find that you have been critical of yourself for so many years that you don't even realize that you are doing it. It is like a default setting. Meditation has helped me, and it can help you be more aware of these negative or limiting thoughts, and to let go of them along with the story lines that may have been in your mind for years.

None of us would choose to stay in a negative thought pattern. Max Lucado, in his book, *Anxious for Nothing* says, "Do you want to guarantee tomorrow's misery? Then wallow in a mental mud pit of self-pity or guilt or anxiety today. (Assume the worst. Beat yourself up. Rehearse your regrets. Complain to complainers.) Thoughts have consequences."[49]

To quote from Dr. Amen again, he has named these thoughts ANTS or Automatic Negative Thinking. Amen says, "You can train your thoughts to be positive and hopeful or you can just allow them to be negative and upset you." If you can learn to recognize the negative thoughts as they come, you can correct them and take their power away from you.[50]

Meditation has helped me to become aware of how I am feeling and then to face those feelings – whether they are positive or negative. This newly found self-awareness of my emotions allows me to combat stressful situations I encounter throughout the day. You know the feeling – something happens that causes you to be upset, and as you get in tune with your feelings, you recognize that your mind and body are going to a place of stress. Your heart may race. You start breathing heavier, or you may find yourself not breathing properly. Now that I am more aware, when this happens I can take my own time out to get back in a better state of mind. Once I do this, I can think more objectively again, and take action to resolve an issue.

Meditation Tips

I have come a long way since that first meditation practice. It has now become part of my regular morning routine, as familiar as making my first cup of coffee. Brain training techniques have improved my outlook, my memory, my focus, and creativity. Simply put, I have learned to become mindful, and you can too. With healthy minds, we can have healthy lives.

I can't claim to be an expert in meditation but will offer some tips that have helped me along the way:

- **Declare your intent.** Knowing and declaring the intent of your practice each day is helpful in achieving the most with it. Why are you meditating? Some days the answer will be very specific, such as you want to quiet anxiety or another strong emotion; you are seeking clarity; or you desire creativity for a project. Other days there may not be anything that comes to mind and your intent will be more generic.

- **Allow your thoughts to come and go.** I used to think that the many thoughts going through my brain were bad and it was my job to stop them. Instead, I had to learn to accept that this is ok, and normal. Let your thoughts come freely, and then simply let them pass by. I like the analogy of a blue sky, and that our thoughts are the clouds floating around. We can notice the clouds and just let them be there, and then go on their way.

- **Know you will get distracted.** With the expectation that various thoughts will arise during your practice, part of meditation is training your brain to be more aware. A helpful mantra for this is using the 3 R's: Recognize, Release, Return. Recognize when you are having a distracting thought. Release the thought. Then, return to your meditation routine.

- **Track your progress.** With every new habit, tracking it is the sure way to make it stick. Find the best time of day to incorporate a meditation practice – even if it is only three to five minutes to begin with – just start it and track it. Evaluate each week how it is working for you and adjust as necessary.

Sometimes you will find during the day that your "monkey brain" appears out of nowhere. When this happens, make the time to stop and take a break. This is the only way to train the mind to quiet down. You may think, as I used to, that you are *too* busy to do this. You are behind. You have a pressing deadline. You feel overwhelmed. In times of extreme pressure, it is even more important to stop.

Try this simple exercise to calm your mind:

1. **Find a Quiet Spot.** Go where you won't be interrupted for ten minutes. Be assured these ten minutes will not be wasted – in fact you will triple them in productivity.

2. **Make Yourself Comfortable.** Take a comfortable position – you can be sitting up or lying down. Close your eyes.

3. **Breathe.** Start with three deep cleansing breaths, in through the nose and out through the mouth. Are you breathing properly? When you breathe in, you should feel your chest and abdomen expanding, and

when you breathe out, expel all the air out like a collapsed balloon. If this is difficult, place your hand on your stomach and you should feel the stomach rise with your in-breath and flatten with your exhale. It helps me to count the breaths – in for a count of 4, hold for 2, out for a count of 8.

4. **Open your senses to the sounds around you**. Listen, differentiate and name to yourself three different sounds that you hear. Take your time. Now open your physical senses. Feel your body where it touches the surface you are sitting on – your seat heavy on the chair, your arms resting on your lap. Do the same process with all five senses, taking your time to thoughtfully focus on each one.

5. **Let Go**. Now simply let go and let your brain rest for a moment, doing whatever it wants to do. Then bring your focus back to your breathing, ending the exercise with three more cleansing breaths.

Though we can't eliminate the thousands of thoughts that go through our heads each day, we do have the power to train our brains to rest and focus. By taking time to calm your mind, you can eliminate your monkey brain and get back to the task at hand more effectively.

Hopefully you leave this chapter with some new information about the brain and how important it is to your overall well-being. The wandering thoughts and the overwhelmed mind is something that you have power over. As I incorporated meditation into a regular routine, my frenetic mind, prone to chatter, became more like a computer that has been shut down at the end of the day. Instead of the busy desktop with fleeting images, my brain became like the clean and restful screen of a computer in sleep mode.

The wandering thoughts and the overwhelmed mind is something that you have power over.

Train your mind to be calm and you will increase your focus and productivity. I encourage you to incorporate mindfulness into your life and you will improve your peace of mind.

"To the mind that is still the whole universe surrenders." – Lao Tzu

EVALUATE YOUR PEACE OF MIND

Ask yourself the following questions:

1. How is your peace of mind?

2. Do you already have a practice for incorporating mindfulness in your life?

3. If so, evaluate how this is working for you and what, if any, changes you would like to make to improve this process.

4. If not, look at adding this to your daily routine. Review the tips on meditation from this chapter to help you.

Challenge Exercise

CALM YOUR BUSY MIND

Try the five-step process in this chapter any time during the day to quiet your mind and increase your focus and productivity.

1. Find a Quiet Spot. Go where you won't be interrupted for ten minutes. Be assured these ten minutes will not be wasted – in fact you will triple them in productivity.

2. Make Yourself Comfortable. Take a comfortable position – you can be sitting up or lying down. Close your eyes.

3. Breathe. Start with three deep cleansing breaths, in through the nose and out through the mouth. Are you breathing properly? When you breathe in, you should feel your chest and abdomen expanding, and when you breathe out, expel all the air out like a collapsed balloon. If this is difficult, place your hand on your stomach and you should feel the stomach rise with your in-breath and flatten with your

exhale. It helps me to count the breaths – in for a count of 4, hold for 2, out for a count of 8.

4. Open your senses to the sounds around you. Listen, differentiate and name to yourself three different sounds that you hear. Take your time. Now open your physical senses. Feel your body where it touches the surface you are sitting on – your seat heavy on the chair, your arms resting on your lap. Do the same process with all five senses, taking your time to thoughtfully focus on each one.

5. Let Go. Now simply let go and let your brain rest for a moment, doing whatever it wants to do. Then bring your focus back to your breathing, ending the exercise with three more cleansing breaths.

Chapter 15

SUCCESS BODY

"Why settle for good health when you can have great health?"

In the early morning light, the mist rising over Lake Alta in the world-renowned resort of Whistler, British Columbia, created a breathtaking scene. However, it wasn't the usual quiet morning you would find on this pristine lake in late summer.

This morning the energy was palpable as close to 3,000 athletes got ready to take to the water for the first leg of the Ironman Canada Race. This challenging triathlon is the most recognized endurance race in the world and features three different disciplines: starting with a 2.4-mile swim; followed by a 112-mile bike ride; and finally a full marathon

– 26.2 miles. Many of these athletes train year around for this event to be ready for the physical toll it takes to complete. This year my husband Graham was one of the contenders.

When the starting gun went off, the few thousand people doing the race all rushed the water and began to swim. It was unnerving for me to watch (actually a bit terrifying) as it was a quick and chaotic mass of arms and legs flailing about as swimmers jockeyed for their best position. Losing Graham from my sights immediately, I scanned the water, watching the swimmers and praying he did not get kicked in the head and drown out there. It was an immense relief when I recognized him coming out of the water over an hour later with a smile on his face – one event down, two to go. The athletes skimmed out of their wet suits and hopped on their bikes. Graham was obviously ready to tackle the next event – the long bike ride – as it is his strong suit.

I followed the racers alongside the course and cheered them on. At one point I met up with Graham's training coach and we were like proud parents chatting up our star athlete, so excited when we were able to spot him on the course and yell out our support. After a long day, I stood at the end of the finish stage watching for Graham to come around the last bend. There were far too many people wearing red and I couldn't tell which one was him. At last, there he was, and tears sprung to my eyes as I watched him run the final stretch of the race to cross the finish line. Months of training and personal sacrifice culminated in an amazing moment when the announcer stated, "Graham Youtsey, you are an Ironman."

Being able to participate as a support person for my husband was an amazing experience. Throughout the day, as I followed the racers, I was mesmerized and awed by the unbelievable feat these individuals had signed up for. Having supported my husband through months and months of training, I found the drive, discipline and passion of these athletes not just admirable, but incredible.

The qualities of drive, discipline and passion are not limited just to athletes. I recognize these attributes in many of my business colleagues. Just like these dedicated athletes, strong business entrepreneurs and executives are "corporate athletes" who desire to be peak performers – not on the race field but in their lives and their businesses.

Brad Stulberg and Steve Magness, in their book, *Peak Performance,* talk about top performers. "Whether it's a writer preparing to draft a story, an athlete prepping for a competition, or a businessperson heading into a high-stakes presentation, great performers never just *hope* they'll be on top of their game. Rather, they actively create the specific conditions that will elicit their personal best." [51]

This book has provided a holistic approach to creating your best life and I would be remiss if I didn't dedicate a chapter to health. Why? Our health is one of the key areas of life we need to manage in order to have optimum performance personally and professionally. By managing your physical energy through 1. Proper Nutrition 2. Exercise, and 3. Sleep, you will maximize your productivity and enhance your well-being. In this chapter I would like to teach you some of the principles I have learned to improve my health in these three specific areas. Then in the challenge section of this chapter you can rate your own health and set goals in the areas you would like to improve.

Our health is one of the key areas of life we need to manage in order to have optimum performance personally and professionally.

You Are What You Eat

The first health component of optimal performance I would like to review is nutrition. Nutrition is foundational to good health. Maslow, in his pyramid depicting the five-tier model of human needs, has nutrition listed at the base. Along with proper rest, food and water are the most basic needs for physical survival. "If these needs are not satisfied the human body cannot function optimally. Maslow considered physiological needs the most important as all the other needs become secondary until these needs are met."[52]

These basic needs are critical, yet often downplayed by business leaders. In my work, I have found that the majority of leaders show little attention to their physical health. This important foundation is often neglected, while we work on the upper levels of the pyramid toward self-actualization.

Recently I brought in an International Sports Sciences Association (ISSA) certified fitness and nutrition coach to my leadership group as a guest speaker. She talked with us about the importance of nutrition and the mistake people make of using willpower versus habits. Willpower doesn't work. Similar to the way you need to create healthy habits and routines for your productivity at work, you should create habits for good sustainable health.

When her clients come to her wanting to lose weight, she shows them how to incorporate healthy nutritional habits into their lives. We can only avoid bad food habits with willpower for so long. Eventually, in a weak moment, we will give in. "You can wipe out one hour of exercise in five minutes with a bad food choice."[53] However, if you create a healthy habit that becomes a ritual each day, it will be much more effective. You want the habit to be as automatic as brushing your teeth – you don't even think about it.

A nutritionist I worked with to help me get on track suggested a few simple habits that I have incorporated:

1. *Have a colorful plate at every meal.* Typically, if we have a bland color palate we tend to be missing foods from some of the food groups. "Color" is usually reflected in the various bright vegetables and fruit that we add to our plates. Some of my favorites that give a lot of "bang for the buck" are blueberries, beets, colorful peppers, broccoli, and varied mixed greens.

2. *Limit myself to one carbohydrate per meal.* Carbohydrates tend to be my weak spot (I love delicious homemade bread and pasta) so I pick just one. If I am having bread I skip the rice.

3. *Have a handful of nuts.* Heathy nuts such as almonds and walnuts are a great source of protein and oils. I will add nuts to my salad and keep small packages in my car for a quick snack.

How Our Bodies Use Energy

One of the most interesting things I learned in studying nutrition was about how our bodies use what we eat, along with how we expend energy throughout the day. Consider this chart provided by the US National Library of Medicine.

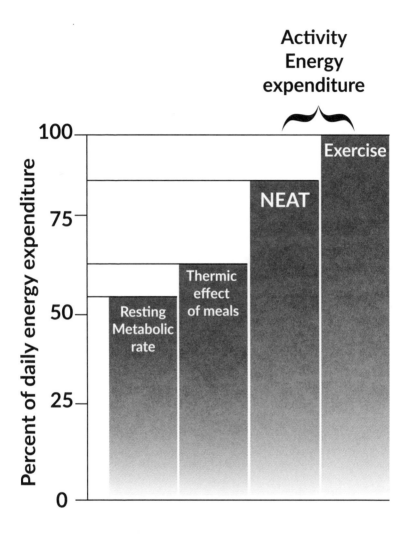

Our resting metabolic rate (RMR), which is the largest section on the chart accounts for over 50 percent of our daily energy expenditure. RMR is the energy associated with the maintenance of major body functions. The thermal effect of food (TEF) uses 10 percent of the total. Activity energy expenditure (AEE) is the most variable component and can be divided into exercise and non-exercise activity thermogenesis (NEAT). Together they can account for 20-40 percent of the total.[54]

NEAT is the energy expended for everything we do that is not sleeping, eating or sports-like exercise. It ranges from the energy expended walking to work, typing, performing yard work, undertaking agricultural tasks and fidgeting. According to a journal published by the American Heart Association, NEAT varies by up to 2000 kcal per day between people of similar size in part because of the substantial variation in the amount of activity that they perform. Obesity is associated with low NEAT; according to some studies, obese individuals stand and ambulate for 2.5 hours per day less than lean sedentary controls. Because walking even at slow velocities is highly exothermic, the NEAT deficit in obesity is likely to be energetically important."[55]

What I found so fascinating about NEAT was our ability to control and increase this non-exercise activity throughout the day. You can see from the graph the impact that various non-exercise activities can have on our energy burn throughout the day.

% Increase above rest

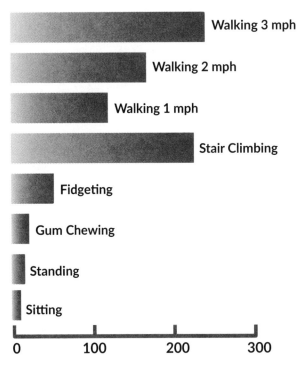

Have you ever sat next to the person that is constantly tapping their foot or bouncing their leg – they are burning calories through their fidgeting! With an increasing number of us having jobs where we need to sit all day, it takes a conscious effort to get up and promote an active lifestyle. The positive impact of these non-exercise activities is that with minimal effort we can add some of them into our work day and immediately see a difference.

Here are a few ways I have incorporated the conventional wisdom of "moving more" into my daily routine:

1. **Stand up while while you work.** Add a stand-up desk where you can vary sitting and standing throughout the day.
2. **Have walking meetings.** Rather than sitting in a conference room, schedule some of your meetings on a walk.
3. **Take frequent moving breaks.** At least once an hour, stand up and take a stretch and move around – visit a co-worker, use the restroom or kitchen that is further from your office.
4. **Use the stairs.** Whenever possible, avoid the elevators and escalators and take the stairs.
5. **Park far away.** Rather than taking the front parking space at the gym, the grocery store or the shopping center, park further away and give yourself more steps.

Exercise Like It's Your job

The second component of optimum health is regular exercise. You know exercise is good for you, but it can be difficult to maintain a regular routine. Here are a few reminders of why it is so important:

- Regular physical activity can improve your muscle strength and boost your endurance.

- Exercise delivers oxygen and nutrients to your tissues and helps your cardiovascular system work more efficiently.

- When your heart and lung health improve, you have more energy to tackle daily chores.[56]

A very good book that helped "kick me in the butt" to exercise on a regular basis was, *Younger Next Year: Live Strong, Fit, and Sexy – Until You're 80 and Beyond,* by Chris Crowley and Dr. Henry S. Lodge. There is a male and female version of the book. My husband chose to read my female version – go figure. Dr. Lodge, or "Harry" as Chris calls him, tells us this:

"Biologically, there is no such thing as retirement, or even aging. There is only growth or decay, and your body looks to you to choose between them."[57] When we exercise, it triggers messages to "grow" to our mind and body. Dr. Lodge gives the strong message to be active through various types of exercise six days a week for the rest of our lives.[58]

As soon as we start to exercise, our body will turn on growth signals that will overwhelm the signals to atrophy. When done properly, it will begin to build up the muscles, heart, bones, joints, and coordination. We will feel better and have more energy; and ultimately, exercise could help us to live longer lives. With all the advances of modern medicine, if we are reasonably healthy at the age of 50 years old, we are likely to live to 100 or even beyond. Do we want to live today and in later years strong and healthy, or do we want to be in pain and unable to walk without a cane or walker? I, for one, would like to have lots of energy, strength and stamina to do the things I want to do for years to come.

The book details evidence-based benefits to regular exercise. Dr. Lodge states, "It (exercise) leads directly to the younger life we are promising, with its heightened immune system; its better sleep; its weight loss, insulin regulation and fat burning; its improved sexuality; its dramatic resistance to heart attack, stroke, hypertension, Alzheimer's disease, arthritis, osteoporosis, diabetes, high cholesterol and depression. All that comes from exercise. But let your muscles sit idle and decay takes over again."[59]

Taking care of your health through exercise is one of the most important things you can do for yourself.

I have found that exercise is a great way to feel better, and it can be fun too. Taking care of your health through exercise is one of the most important things you can do for yourself. We talked about the importance of calendaring and routines in earlier chapters, and exercise is one of those important priorities that goes right on my calendar as blocked time just like other appointments. We need to exercise like it's our job. Change up the routine from time to time to keep motivated. There are so many options, from walking to running, hiking to skiing, a boot camp class with friends or a competitive Peloton bike challenge with hundreds of people streaming live. We really have no excuse.

Work hard, then Recover

To be in optimal physical condition you need to work hard. This requires committing to a regular workout routine that involves getting your heart rate up. I typically aim for cardio activity five to six days a week, and strength training 2 days a week. Generally, aim for at least 30 minutes of physical activity every day. The Department of Health and Human Services recommends the following guidelines:

- *Aerobic Activity.* At least 150 minutes of moderate aerobic activity or 75 minutes of vigorous activity a week, or a combination of both.

- *Strength Training.* A strength routine of all major muscle groups at least two times a week.[60]

(These will vary depending on your age and your fitness goals. Consult with your doctor to determine what is the right program for you.)

You need to work hard to build your physical fitness and then recover. Balancing work and recovery can be a challenge. In

Chapter 10, we talked about how important it is to take time for rest and renewal. It is critical to recharge and "refill our buckets" of physical, emotional, mental and spiritual health. Remember, you can't pour from an empty glass.

To quote from Loehr and Schwartz again, "Nearly every elite athlete we have worked with over the years has come to us with performance problems that could be traced to an imbalance between the expenditure and the recovery of energy. When we expend energy, we draw down our reservoir. When we recover energy, we fill it back up. Too much energy expenditure without sufficient recovery eventually leads to burnout and breakdown. (Overuse it and lose it.) Too much recovery without sufficient stress leads to atrophy and weakness. (Use it or lose it.)"[61]

In the last few years I have incorporated yoga into my fitness routine and have found many health benefits by adding this practice. For me, adding this regimen has helped me to find better balance with the recovery piece of my fitness routine. I enjoyed working out hard but would rarely take adequate time for cool down and stretching. Adding yoga moves for as little as 10-15 minutes to the end of my workout routine has greatly improved my flexibility and how my body feels overall.

I attended a wellness retreat at the beginning of this year where yoga was a major part of it. It was a wonderful and refreshing experience and I highly recommend it. Yoga is a natural stress reducer and has been shown to significantly decrease the symptoms of stress and anxiety.[62] Yoga is also an effective way to increase strength and endurance. There are several studies that show the health benefits of yoga. One such study showed that regular practice led to improvements in endurance, strength and flexibility.[63]

Are you Sleeping?

Do you remember the French nursery rhyme "Are you sleeping, are you sleeping, Brother John, Brother John? Morning bells are ringing! Morning bells are ringing! Ding, dang, dong. Ding dang, dong." The song is about a friar who has overslept when he is supposed to be up ringing the bells. The whole point is that the bells are not ringing, because Brother John, who is supposed to ring them, is sleeping. [64]

I can relate to Brother John who may have overslept because he had trouble getting to sleep in the first place or woke up in the wee hours and then finally fell back asleep just before the morning alarm.

The third component of optimum health is sleep. This is one I would like to spend a little more time on with you as sleep has been one of those elusive things I have struggled with off and on during my adult life.

At one particularly frustrating season it seemed I had gone weeks without adequate sleep, resulting in me doggedly dragging myself through my days. My sleep deprivation was causing me to feel hazy throughout the day, lethargic, and unable to focus for long periods of time. I decided it was time to take charge and figure out how to give my body the rest it needs.

I began to research sleep and felt a little better when I discovered that I was not alone in my sleep struggles. Not getting good sleep is a common problem in modern society and affects many people at some time in their lives.[65] People will vary in the actual amounts of sleep needed, and the National Sleep Foundation recommends that the average adult from 18 – 64 years should have between 7 to 9 hours of sleep per night.[66] We are not meeting the mark. According to a Gallup survey, the average adult gets 6.8 hours of sleep per night. 40 percent of Americans get six hours or less of sleep, and 14 percent get five hours or less of sleep per night.[67]

Occasional sleep disruption is normal and generally no more than a nuisance, however ongoing lack of sleep is a problem. See if you recognize any of these symptoms of sleep loss in your own life:

- yawning
- moodiness
- fatigue
- irritability
- depressed mood

- difficulty learning new concepts
- forgetfulness
- inability to concentrate or a "fuzzy" head
- lack of motivation
- clumsiness
- increased appetite and carbohydrate cravings
- reduced sex drive

The National Institute of Health (NIH), in their research on "Brain Basics: Understanding Sleep," noted: "Sleep is an important part of your daily routine – you spend about one-third of your time doing it. Quality sleep – and getting enough of it at the right times – is as essential to survival as food and water. Without sleep you can't form or maintain the pathways in your brain that let you learn and create new memories, and it's harder to concentrate and respond quickly."[68] The NIH study goes on to describe different stages of sleep and their importance as outlined in the following charts.[66]

Sleep Stages

There are two basic types of sleep: rapid eye movement (REM) sleep and non-REM sleep (which has three different stages). Each is linked to specific brain waves and neuronal activity. You cycle through all stages of non-REM and REM sleep several times during a typical night, with increasingly longer, deeper REM periods occurring toward morning.

Stage 1

Non-REM, stage 1 sleep is the changeover from wakefulness to sleep. During this short period (lasting several minutes) of relatively light sleep, your heartbeat, breathing, and eye movements slow, and your muscles relax with occasional twitches. Your brain waves begin to slow from their daytime wakefulness patterns.

Stage 2

Non-REM, stage 2 sleep is a period of light sleep before you enter deeper sleep. Your heartbeat and breathing slow, and muscles relax even further. Your body temperature drops, and eye movements stop. Brain wave activity slows but is marked by brief bursts of electrical activity. You spend more of your repeated sleep cycles in stage 2 sleep than in other sleep stages.

Stage 3

Non-REM, stage 3 sleep is the period of deep sleep that you need to feel refreshed in the morning. It occurs in longer periods during the first half of the night. Your heartbeat and breathing slow to their lowest levels during sleep. Your muscles are relaxed and it may be difficult to awaken you. Brain waves become even slower.

REM sleep

REM sleep first occurs about 90 minutes after falling asleep. Your eyes move rapidly from side to side behind closed eyelids. Mixed frequency brain wave activity becomes closer to that seen in wakefulness. Your breathing becomes faster and irregular, and your heart rate and blood pressure increase to near waking levels. Most of your dreaming occurs during REM sleep, although some can also occur in non-REM sleep. Your arm and leg muscles become temporarily paralyzed, which prevents you from acting out your dreams. As you age, you sleep less of your time in REM sleep. Memory consolidation most likely requires both non-REM and REM sleep.

Better Sleep is Possible

The first step, once you realize that sleep is a problem for you, is to begin keeping a sleep log. You will recall we talked about measuring everything we want to improve earlier in the book – the habit of good sleep is no different. As a first step to improving my sleep I started keeping track of it, writing down how many hours I slept each night and how rested I felt when I woke up. I kept my notes in a journal, and used a sleep app. There are several helpful apps on the market: one of my favorites is the sleep tracker on Fitbit. At first the app only tracked the number of hours I slept each night, but with an upgrade it now tracks the type of sleep I get, including light, deep and REM sleep.

As described on the previous pages, the quality of our sleep is as important as the quantity, so you want to ensure you are getting the proper amount of both deep and REM sleep. I am now so in tune to my body that I know immediately when I wake up whether I have had a solid amount of deep sleep based on how refreshed I feel.

Tracking my sleep and journaling was very helpful as over time I was able to identify patterns. I found that when I didn't sleep well it was often because of how the day had played out; choices I had made hadn't allowed me to properly rest. As an example, if I ended up working late into the evening I had a hard time settling down for the night and sleeping soundly. If I exercised after dinner I tended to have less deep sleep. Conversely, when I had vigorous exercise earlier in the day, I had better sleep.

It took time. I made specific necessary changes and eventually my sleep pattern improved and got to a steady rhythm, where I was getting regular, quality sleep. I created my own sleep disciplines to help keep me on track. If you struggle with sleep issues, try these 10 Tips for Better Sleep:

1. **Have a regular evening routine**. An evening wind down routine prepares your body for a good night's sleep. Refer to Chapter 10 to learn how to create your own.

2. **Set a sleep and wake schedule**. Try to set a schedule where as much as possible you go to bed and get up at the same time each day. When you do this on a regular basis, your body will begin to remember this routine and you'll begin to experience better and more consistent sleep.

3. **Make your bedroom your sanctuary**. Have this sleeping room where you spend so many hours be a place of respite with calming colors, welcoming décor and comfortable bedding. Keep it clean and neat so you are not tripping over clutter to get around.

4. **Shut off the electronics**. We have all heard about the blue light effect that keeps our brains firing. It is

best to eliminate all electronics – TV, computer, and phone – at least one hour before bedtime.

5. **Turn down the temperature**. The body's core temperature needs to drop to initiate sleep, so sleeping in a colder room will result in a better night's sleep.

6. **Block out the light**. Your body's natural rhythm will respond to light as if it is morning and time to get up. Keep your room as dark as possible by investing in black out shades or use a sleep mask.

7. **Block out sound**. As much as possible, create a quiet sleeping space so you are not woken up by noises during the night. If this is difficult, wear ear plugs or try a sleep sounds noise maker. There are several apps on the market that play sleep sounds, or you can purchase a "white noise" machine to put by your bed.

8. **Avoid caffeine and alcohol.** Skip the coffee late in the day, and alcoholic drinks before bed. Everyone is different in how their body handles caffeine. However, I have found that if I eliminate caffeine after dinner and avoid alcoholic drinks before bedtime it helps me to sleep more soundly.

9. **Use essential oils**. There are several essential oils that promote sleep. I like doTerra Essential Oils, in fact my children call me the "witch doctor" because of number of oils I have and bring out for various

remedies. Some of my favorites for sleep are Lavender, Vetiver, Roman Chamomile, and Ylang Ylang.

10. **Check your hormone levels**. Sometimes our sleep issues are caused by a change in our hormones, such as an elevated level of cortisol in our bodies. It's the main stress hormone. Cortisol production is natural and should be high in the morning and lower in the evening. When this out of balance, it can throw off your sleep cycle.

Most of us likely won't be training to be an Ironman like my husband. But if you are, more power to you! However, all of us can commit to taking the best care of our physical selves. As I mentioned before, our health is one of the key areas of life we need to manage in order to have optimum performance personally and professionally.

We only have one body, so I challenge you to evaluate this area of your life and see where you want to make changes to improve your nutrition, your exercise habits, and your sleep.

After all, why settle for good health when you can have great health?

HEALTH BEST PRACTICE

1. What is a current best practice that you have in place for your health and fitness?

2. Now write down a statement of how you will sustain this best practice.

Challenge Exercise

HEALTH ASSESSMENT

Goals	Proper Sleep	Nutrition	Exercise
1 2 3	I struggle to get good sleep and am often tired during the day. Typically sleep less than 5 hours a night.	Eating healthy is not a priority for me. I am significantly over or under weight and not making good food choices.	Exercise is not a priority for me. I do not do cardio or strength training and my body shows it.
4 5 6 7	I enjoy average sleep sometimes feeling well rested and struggle other times with sleeplessness. Typically sleep 5-7 hours per night.	I eat clean and healthy some of the time. Other times I eat junk food. I am not at a healthy weight and my energy is up and down throughout the day.	I am in moderate physical condition and so dome form of activity 3-4 times a week.
8 9 10	I sleep well most all of the time. I wake feeling rested and keep my energy throughout the day. Typically sleep over 7 hours a night.	I look at food as fuel for my body and eat clean and healthy. My weight is on track and I have endless energy.	I am in excellent physical condition and committed to a regular cardio and strength training. I work out 5 or more times a week.
Score			
Goal			

On a scale of 1-10, 1 being poor and 10 being rockstar status, rate yourself in the 3 health areas, Sleep, Nutrition and Exercise. Total your score, then in the next column make an improvement goal for yourself over the next 90 days.

90-Day Health Challenge. In the three areas of Nutrition, Exercise and Sleep described in this chapter, what is one area you would like to focus on in the next 90 days? Write it down now, along with an action item to get started.

Chapter 16

HOW TO GET UNSTUCK

"You alone may lighten this burden or render it intolerable. It is as you choose." Abraham Lincoln

---

It was a beautiful day for a flight. The weather was mild, the skies bright blue, and the airline on time – all indications for smooth travel. I had been anticipating the trip and was excited to be on my way to an industry conference with a great speaker line up.

It was a period of tremendous growth and success in my business. My workload was especially heavy, and I was putting in a lot of hours. At the same time my kids were small, and I felt like every moment not working was spent chaperoning them from one activity to another. My life was full, and I thought I was doing really well. I looked forward to the cross-country flight and getting caught up with some project work and stacked up reading.

Headphones on to one of my favorite music lists I hunkered down.

Sometime later I noticed the flight attendant a few rows ahead taking meal requests. Food sounded great, yes, even airplane food, and I thought about what I would like to order. I might even treat myself to a cocktail. Then a crazy thing happened. The next thing I knew, I looked down and had a meal in front of me, and the flight attendant was a few rows behind. I didn't remember any of it. Not the flight attendant stopping by my seat, not giving my food order, and certainly not the time in between. This was terrifying. Adding to my anxiety was the fact this wasn't the first time I had had a memory lapse in the last six months. In addition, I had also been getting headaches. The headaches were normal, I had been telling myself, but the frequency of them was becoming annoying.

What happened on the flight that day scared me enough to schedule an appointment with the doctor right when I got home. Growing up and still living in the small town of Lynden, Dr. Alexander had been my primary care physician since I was a little girl. Though my first memory of him – not a good one – was resetting several of my toes after a

3-wheeling accident, he had been a steady person in my life through many years. Knowing me well, he asked why I was there, and probed a bit about my work and home life. I let him know everything was going well. Life was extra busy. I was a single mom at the time and had been so for several years, so that was a heavy role but my most important priority. Work was hard but going great and the business was growing. It was just a season in my life and it would get better eventually. The problem was these headaches and memory lapses.

Concerned about the symptoms I was exhibiting, he conducted a full physical, and scheduled a series of lab tests and bloodwork. When these came back within normal ranges he decided to order a brain scan. The week between the scan and my next appointment was admittedly excruciating. I vacillated from "everything is fine" to "I must surely be dying." Fortunately, at my next visit he gave me the great news: My scan was clear. He said to me, "I know you've gone through years of difficulty, you've come through a painful divorce and have been on your own now for several years raising your kids and expanding your business.

Janelle, there is nothing wrong with you physically. You don't need surgery to remove something in your brain, but you need to do drastic surgery on your schedule, because your life and the path you are on need to change."

This conversation was a wakeup call. Sometimes we get off track and don't even know it. This is what happened to me and it can happen to you. It took a health scare for me to realize I had way too much on my plate. I had deceived myself that everything was great, and the business and workload would fix itself on its own. Here I was, the one living the example of life mastery to my friends and colleagues, or so I thought. Although it looked to everyone else, including me, that I had it all together, inside I was dying trying to be Superwoman.

Supermen and Women Don't Exist

Facebook, Instagram and other forms of social media have their perks. I enjoy keeping up with my family across the country – especially seeing all the pictures of my nieces and nephews, who are growing up way too fast. The problem with it, however, is it gives an unrealistic view of life. When we scroll through our feed we see beautiful people with smiling faces, exotic trips, business awards, happy couples, and adorable children, first in their class. We start to feel inadequate and wonder: Why isn't my life like this? Based on this highlight reel of others' amazing lives, we feel we must push hard to have the perfect life, perfect business, perfect marriage, perfect kids.

The quest to be Superwoman brought me to the place I was in – exhausted, distracted, overwhelmed. I kept packing the load heavier and heavier, forgetting myself in the desire to be everything to everyone. That's what I was trying to be and realized it was not sustainable. Though I was experiencing success in some areas, I had sacrificed my body and mind with the heavy load I was under. It was time to stop.

The quest to be Superwoman brought
me to the place I was in – exhausted,
distracted, overwhelmed.

Getting on Track

It was time to stop and that was exactly what I did. Setting a full day of quiet time aside, I painstakingly reviewed my life and revisited my priorities. Though I was involved in many good things, there were just *too* many for me to keep up the pace. I evaluated what things were giving me energy and what things were draining it. Slowly I began to lift commitments off my schedule. It required some tough decisions and learning to say "no" more often. In my evaluation I realized that evening business events were no longer fun but felt like an added chore on top of the workday. They were also taking me away from being with my girls – a top priority for me. I decided to eliminate these afterhours events and meetings in order to be home for dinner and family time each night. Looking at my daily work calendar, it became obvious I had too much on my plate, and it was time for me to hire some additional management help in my business to take some of my work load. I also stepped down from a regular weekend commitment in my community to allow more free time in my schedule. By taking some tasks off my calendar, I was able to schedule some appointments to take better care of myself like recommitting to a daily exercise routine, quiet time, and treating myself to an occasional massage.

Prioritizing what was most important in my life – putting that first and saying "no" to everything else – put me back in the driver's seat once again. I made the necessary choices and was back in control of my life.

Prioritizing what was most important in my life – putting that first and saying "no" to everything else – put me back in the driver's seat.

The change was transformational. I lowered my stress by focusing on the few things that really mattered. As a result, my health improved, my energy increased, and the headaches and memory lapses eventually went away. The reduced commitments allowed me to be more present with my family and friends, and my business continued to grow strong.

I have shared in this chapter a personal story of how I got off track to show that it is so easy to get caught up in the success lie. We work hard, we give a lot, then we give more, and if we are not careful we can sacrifice too much – like I ended up doing with my own health. The time out I gave myself was not a onetime solution. Creating regular reflection time and the various disciplines we have been reviewing together have helped me to stay on track. Learning how to "say no" became so important to me I dedicated a chapter in this book to it. Now I can see more quickly when I am falling into some old destructive habits – which invariably I will. We are, in fact, human – versus Superman or Superwoman. The tools I have shared throughout this book keep me focused and on track, and they can do the same for you.

EVALUATE WHERE YOU MAY BE STUCK

Ask yourself the following questions:

1. As you read this chapter, were you able to relate to a time or area in your life where you had gotten off track from what is most important to you? How did you get there?

2. And most importantly, how did you or will you get yourself back on track?

3. Now that you have identified where you tend to get stuck, how can you prevent yourself from this behavior in the future? Make a list of three or four best practices that you do already or can implement to sustain your success.

Chapter 17

FIND YOUR TRUTH

"Although no one can go back and make a brand new start, anyone can start from now and make a brand new ending." Zig Ziglar

---

The end of the school year brings excitement for many – a time of graduation. This year we celebrated two graduates in our home, with one daughter completing High School and another completing University.

I had the privilege of being the Commencement Speaker at my daughter Paige's High School graduation. I asked the students, "What are you going to do after High School?" This is one of the most asked questions of High School graduates. Over and over people will ask them, "What are you doing after graduation? Where are you going to college? What are you going to do with your life?"

In the short time we had together I asked them a much bigger question,

"What are you going to do to live your BEST life?"

I shared a few words of wisdom with the students – advice that can serve as a good reminder to each of us. As we've talked about throughout this book, our life is made up of our choices – those things big and small that we chose to do or not do. None of us can go backward and change the past.

However, we all can go forward and choose to live intentionally from this point forward, to take charge and design our best lives.

Together we have uncovered the success lie, and reviewed truths that have the power to transform your life, your career, and your mind. You now have a roadmap to create the life you have always wanted.

Right about now your head may be spinning from all the information I have provided throughout the book. That is why we have created a tool to summarize the process called the Leader's Success Plan Summary. It can be found at the end of the book, or you may download a free copy at TheSuccessLie.com. Using the Success Plan Summary, let me help you put it all together:

1. **Take Inventory**. First, you identified where you are living on automatic, and the gap – the space between what is and what could be. You have thought about what you want your legacy to be and have decided to choose the best path ahead – one that will not leave you with regrets. On the Success Plan Summary write down in the first block titled The Gap, three areas you identified from Chapter 3 - Living on Automatic. If you haven't already, take the Success Life Assessment to help you define the areas of your life that you want to improve. Next, in Your Legacy block write down three things you want to be remembered for. Go back to the End in Mind Reflection exercise in Chapter 4 - Start with the End if you need to refresh your memory.

2. **Identify your values and live by your priorities**. In Chapter 5 – The Juggling Act, you identified or reviewed your values – the "why" of your life. You are here on earth for a purpose, with different gifts and talents that you are called to use to reach your full potential. Finding out what those are is your personal mission. In the next block Your Values, write down your top three values from the Core Values Assessment at the end of Chapter 5. Then in the block Your Priorities write in your top three priorities. I want to remind you that these are your main areas of focus and what you should be spending the majority

of your time on. Ask yourself the question on each priority, "Does this priority align with your values?"

3. **The Difficulty Challenge**. How you show up is critical to your success. You will undoubtedly face difficult situations, but you can control your response. In fact, with the right perspective these times can propel you to a level of growth you could not have otherwise achieved. Go back and review the Defining Moments Reflection from Chapter 6 – Bitter or Better. Ask yourself these questions: "How will you respond to the next challenge you face?" "What type of attitude and perspective do you want to have?" In the Perspective block, write down the top three responses you will choose to have as you encounter a problem.

4. **The Peak Performer**. You may have already implemented some of the success tools and routines you have learned in this book to increase productivity, do more in less time, and create the space in your life for your most important priorities. In Your Goals block, write down the top three goals you want to accomplish over the next year. Listing your top goals on your summary sheet is an easy way to check in from time to time to see if you are on track with them. Use the more detailed Success Goals Outline from Chapter 7 – Goal Setting Success to provide a detailed action plan and accountability. Next, on Your

Habits block, list three habits you want to implement to assist you in achieving your goals. Would you like to better manage your email, create a morning routine, or challenge yourself to unplug? Refer back to Section Two – Transform Your Career for ideas.

5. **Be the Overcomer**. In Part Three you learned what gets in the way of leading and living your best life, as well as what steps you can take to improve your self-awareness, and eliminate barriers hindering your success. You have discovered the power of your brain, and how to train it along with your body to maximize your productivity and enhance your well-being. You also realize that, even with the best intentions, you will get stuck now and then. In The Barriers block, write down the three main things that tend to trip you up. Being aware of these potential roadblocks will help you to be prepared with a plan to overcome them when they rear their heads. In the final block, the Result, take time to visualize yourself achieving true success. Write down how you will feel once you have created that success and are living the life you have always wanted.

Don't be Afraid to Fall

One last piece of advice I have for designing your best life is don't be afraid of the times you will get off track, and the times you will fall. You are human and no matter your best intention, there will be times when you make the wrong decision, miss an important goal, or fail a loved one. There are times you are going to get off track and times you will simply fall. Accept that this will happen and realize failure can lead to success.

I have fallen so many times in my life, personally and professionally. As I have described in previous chapters there have been far more learnings in the challenging times than at any other time. You may have faced significant challenges in your life as well. These can be a deterrent, but don't have to destroy you. You can overcome and choose to allow these situations to shape you to be better than ever.

As an example, my grandson Korbin learned to walk recently. He was not really interested in learning to walk, so we turned into enthusiastic fans cheering him on when he decided to attempt for the first time. His brother Willem balanced him on his feet and with a determined look on his face Korbin did the "drunken sailor walk" to us—three whole steps, and then he fell on his bottom. He looked up at us with a big grin. Did we get upset with him for falling? No! We clapped and cheered, and Korbin did too. It didn't matter that he had fallen; it was progress. He had walked!

Take the First Step

As we complete this journey together, you are taking a first step. As you follow the plan for your life there will be times that you are overwhelmed; and times that you fall and get back up again. My faith has guided me through these times and one of my favorite verses is in Psalm 32. "I will guide you along the best pathway for your life. I will advise you and watch over you."

To live the life of significance you were born for, the life you have always wanted, it is up to you to make the decision to take charge. Let go of the Success Lie and Find Your Truth. Discover your purpose, that purpose which is uniquely yours and will have the most positive impact on your family, your community, your world.

> Choose to live intentionally. Take charge and design your best life.

Wherever you are in life, you are taking first steps. Choose to live intentionally. Take charge and design your best life. Utilize the Success Plan you have created as your road map. Do the work and gain control. Take a step, and don't be afraid to fall. Learn and grow.

The decision is yours. No one can do it for you. It's up to you.

What are you going to do to live your best life?

Success Plan Summary

The Gap

1.
2.
3.

Your Legacy

1.
2.
3.

Your Priorities

1.
2.
3.

Your Values

1.
2.
3.

Your Perspective

1.
2.
3.

Your Goals

1.
2.
3.

Your Barriers

1.
2.
3.

Your Habits

1.
2.
3.

The Result

1.
2.
3.

Afterword

Congratulations on completing *The Success Lie*. You have the desire to let go of the modern world's path to success to create a life of fulfillment and true significance instead. My hope is through the reading of this book you have uncovered your success lies and are ready to commit to building your best life – one that you design.

As you have likely found, the concepts I have provided are relatively easy and many of them you probably already know. The key is not the knowing but the willingness and discipline to do the work, and to do it consistently until a habit develops. Building the skills I suggest are not developed overnight. Like Olympic athletes who work for years before the games, it takes time to build the skills necessary for success. The good news is that everything I suggest in this book is learnable if you are committed and willing to invest the time. By taking an intentional approach, you can use the Leader's Success Plan Summary to take control, perform and lead more effectively.

If you need help putting it all together, that is what we do at Legacy Leader. Our certified specialists can walk you through step by step, and help you set up your own personal system of mastery. We can help train you and your teams.

By applying the lessons in *The Success Lie*, you will discover the life you have always wanted becomes the life you are living. You will find out that you can overcome overwhelm and achieve peace of mind.

This book is dedicated to the entrepreneur, the one who has crazy ideas and puts their head, heart, and hard-earned cash on the line. The one that goes "all-in." Who then takes others along for the ride and when done right, not only creates a life of joy for themselves but a life of significance that is far beyond themselves and their families, a legacy of impact in their communities and the world.

To your success!

Resources to Help You Overcome Overwhelm

Book Janelle to energize and inspire your group. Go to www.JanelleBruland.com or www.TheSuccessLie.com for speaking engagement information.

Take the Life Assessment to get a baseline on where you are currently living on automatic and start the process to take your life back. Go to www.TheSuccessLie.com to download this and other resources to help you design your best life.

Utilize our Leadership Coaching Program to break through barriers to transform your leadership, crush your goals, and love your life.

Join one of our Leadership Mastermind Groups or Facebook Community to connect with other elite professionals to share best practices and grow in your unique calling of leadership.

Attend one of our Training Workshops or the join the Leader's Success Academy to learn how to implement the concepts and tools in *The Success Lie*.

For questions about any of these strategies or investments please contact us at:

www.TheSuccessLie.com

Info@TheSuccessLie.com

Acknowledgements

Writing a book is no small task, and for me, it has been a journey of over five years to put the thoughts together into a completed manuscript. I had no idea when I began this process how hard it would be, how long it would take, and the number of people that would support me along the way. I didn't think of my story as remarkable. It wasn't until several people had let me know that my overcoming challenges had inspired them to make changes in their own lives that I began to have thoughts that maybe this was something I was supposed to do. I realized that even though there were times of complete overwhelm where problems seemed insurmountable, I got through them and grew through the process. If I could do it, surely others could too, and I needed to tell them how.

This book is the result of a team effort, not only through the writing and publication process, but all the help and lessons learned along the way from colleagues, co-workers, friends, and family throughout my many years as an entrepreneur. I want to acknowledge those people who have been instrumental in my life.

First, the love and support of my parents, Don and Janice. I don't think you quite knew what to do with this creative, high energy daughter of yours, you nevertheless encouraged and supported me unconditionally. You set a wonderful example of staying true to what's important and have always given me the emotional safety net I needed to take risks and chase dreams.

I thank my family, our children, and grandchildren for your love and being the greatest joy of my life. A special thanks to my three daughters, Terell, Payton and Paige for your love and support, and for being my biggest cheerleaders and fans. I couldn't be prouder of each of you, and you inspire me every day with your courage, compassion, and desire to change the world.

Thank you to my biggest supporter and best friend, my husband Graham. For your love, your unwavering commitment to me, our children, and grandchildren, for the countless times you listened and encouraged me through my many thoughts, ideas, and swirling emotions of this experience, I can't adequately express my appreciation.

Next, I offer sincere gratitude to my team at MSNW. The work ethic, grit, passion and care you display every day has taken our company from ordinary to extraordinary. Getting to work alongside such dedicated, energetic people and growing together over the last two decades has been an incredible experience. Thank you to my marketing specialist Heather for "kicking me in the backside" to start writing, and to Terell and my superstar management team for allowing me to take the time needed to focus on this book project. You are all amazing.

I thank the many clients whom I've worked with over the years and for your trust and partnership. To my colleagues at Leadership and Executive Edge, you inspire me with your insatiable desire for growth and impact.

I am thankful for the many friends, mentors, and supporters in my life. For my dearest friends, who wish I would slow down a bit but still love me just as I am. For my fellow entrepreneurs and friends at Building Service Contractors Association. For Pastor Ken, my constant encourager, who walked with me through the highest highs and lowest lows of my life. And for Pastor Kim, who challenged me to make the necessary endings to pursue a bigger calling.

I want to say a special thank you to my wonderful publishers Bryan and DeeDee Heathman and your fantastic team at Made for Success Publishing for your tireless commitment to me, and to making this book project be its very best. Thank you to Michelle Prince for getting me started on the road to publishing and to my elite editors Judy Slack and Alexandra Twin for your enthusiasm and support. You made the book infinitely better with your feedback.

Finally, and most important of all, I thank God for giving me the gifts and passion for pursuing my calling of leadership, and the endurance to complete this work. To Him be the glory.

Endnotes

1 Dweck, Dr. Carol, Mindset – The New Psychology of Success (New York: Ballantine Books) 2006, 46

2 ibid, 16

3 Maxwell, John C. *The 15 Invaluable Laws of Growth*. New York: Center Street, 2012.

4 Sigmund Freud – Biography; Unconscious Mind, Saul McLeod, Simply Psychology; The Unconscious Mind, JA Bargh, NCBI National Institutes of Health.

5 Mary Helen Immordino-Yang, Joanna A. Christodoulou, Vanessa Singh. (2012, June 29) Rest Is Not Idleness -Implications of the Brain's Default Mode for Human Development and Education. Perspectives on Psychological Science. Association for Psychological Science.

6 Gutzler, Steve. The Leader's Legacy. Leadership Edge Retreat, La Jolla, CA, September 13, 2018

7 Ware, Bronnie. *The Top Five Regrets of the Dying* (Australia: Hay House, Inc.) 2012

8 ibid, 37

9 ibid, 43

10 ibid, 70

11 ibid, 102

12 ibid, 135

13 ibid, 167

14 Parker J. Palmer. *Let Your Life Speak: Listening for the Voice of Vocation*. (New York: John Wiley & Sons, Inc.) 2000, 76

15 Parker J. Palmer. *Let Your Life Speak: Listening for the Voice of Vocation*. (New York: John Wiley & Sons, Inc.) 2000, 628, 121.

16 O'Donahue, John. *To Bless the Space Between Us*. (pg. 146) New York: Doubleday, 2008.

17 Loehr, Jim. Schwartz, Tony. *The Power of Full Engagement*. New York: Simon & Schuster, Inc.,2005, 23

18 Gladwell, Malcolm. *David and Goliath*. New York: Little, Brown and Company, 2013.

19 Nietzsche, Friedrich. *Twilight of the Idols*. Germany, London: 1990 Penguin Classics, 1889

20 Shpancer, Noam Ph.D. (August, 2010). What Doesn't Kill You Makes You Weaker. *Psychology Today*.

21 Statistic Brain Research Institute. (2018, January 9). New Year's Resolution Statistics

22 ibid

23 Aronson, Elliot and Eugene Gerard. "Beyond Parkinson's Law: The Effect of Excess Time on Subsequent Performance." Journal of Personality and Social Psychology, vol. 3, no. 3, Mar. 1966, pp. 336-339. EBSCOhost, doi:10.1037/h0023000.

24 Dinsmore, Scott. *Warren Buffett's 5-Step Process for Prioritizing True Success*. Live Your Legend. Feb 1, 2016

25 Collins, Jim. *Good to Great*. New York: HarperCollins Publishers, Inc., 2001. 139

26 Loehr, Jim. Schwartz, Tony. *The Power of Full Engagement*. New York: Simon & Schuster, Inc.,2005.

27 IDC Study: Mobile and Social Connectiveness (2013, April) IDC Research.

28 John Assaraf and Murray Smith, *The Answer: Grow Any Business, Achieve Financial Freedom, and Live an Extraordinary Life* (New York: Atria Books, 2008), 50.

29 Nomura, Catherine. Waller, Julia. Waller, Shannon. *Unique Ability: Creating the Life You Want* (Toronto Canada: The Strategic Coach Inc. 2003). 25.

30 Wingate, Lisa. *Before We Were Yours*. New York: Penguin Random House. 2017

31 Carnegie, Dale. *How to Stop Worrying and Start Living*. (New York: Simon & Schuster Inc., 1944). 18

32 ibid, 16-18

33 ibid, 18

34 Lucado, Max. *Anxious for Nothing: Finding Calm in a Chaotic World*. (Nashville, TN: Thomas Nelson. 2017) 151

35 Givray,Henry. SmithBucklin Leadership Institute. March 7, 2014. SmithBucklin, Chicago, IL

36 Robb O'Hagen, Sarah. Extreme You. BSCAI Contracting Success, September, 2017, Bellagio Hotel, Las Vegas, NV. Keynote.

37 Amen, Dr. Daniel G. *Change Your Brain, Change Your Life*. New York: Three Rivers Press, 1996. 25

38 ibid, 29

39 Wallis, Claudia (1983, June 6) Can we Cope? Time Magazine

40 American Psychological Association (2017). *Stress in America: The state of our nation.* Stress in America™ Survey. 4

41 ibid, 16

42 ibid, 14-16

43 UC Berkeley, Molecular Psychiatry, 2/11/14

44 Psychiatry Research 262 (2018) 232-332

45 Killingsworth, Matthew A. Gilbert, Daniel T. (2010, November). A Wandering Mind Is an Unhappy Mind. Journal of Science. Harvard University, 932.

46 Lucado, Max. *Anxious for Nothing.* Nashville, Tennessee: Thomas Nelson. 1679

47 Amen, Dr. Daniel G. *Change Your Brain, Change Your Life.* New York: Three Rivers Press, 1996. 112

48 Brad Stulberg, Steve Magness. **Peak Performance**. New York: Rodale Inc., 2017, 125

49 Saul McLeod (2018, May) Maslow's Hierarchy of Needs. Simply Psychology.

50 Coraleigh Jones (2018, July) 6 Habits of Healthy Bodies. Leadership Edge meeting, Woodinville, WA

51 Todd M. Manini (2010, January 9) Energy Expenditure and Aging. PMC. US National Library of Medicine

52 James A. Levine, Mark W. Vander Weg, James O. Hill, Robert C. Klesges (2006, January 18). Non-Exercise Activity Thermogenesis. The Crouching Tiger Hidden Dragon of Societal Weight Gain. American Heart Association, Inc.

53 Mayo Clinic. (2016, October 30) Exercise: 7 benefits of regular physical activity. Healthy Lifestyle Fitness.

54 Chris Crowley, Dr. Henry S. Lodge. *Younger Next Year: Live Strong, Fit, and Sexy – Until You're 80 and Beyond*. New York: Workman Publishing. 2005, 70

55 ibid, 51

56 ibid, 71

57 Laskowski, Dr. Edward R. (2016, August 20) How much should the average adult exercise every day? Healthy Lifestyle Fitness. Mayo Clinic

58 Loehr, Jim. Schwartz, Tony. *The Power of Full Engagement*. New York: Simon & Schuster, Inc.,2005, 29

59 Li AW. (2012, March 17) The Effects of Yoga on Anxiety and Stress. Altern Med Rev. 21-35

60 Caren Lau, Ruby Yu, Jean Woo (2015, June 8) Effects of a 12-Week Hatha Yoga Intervention on Cardiorespiratory Endurance, Muscular Strength and Endurance, and Flexibility in Hong Kong Chinese Adults: A Controlled Clinical Trial. Evidence-based Complementary and Alternative Medicine. 958727

61 David S. Landes, *The wealth and poverty of nations*, W.W. Norton, NY, London, 1998, p. 48

62 Kathleen Davis FNP. (2018, January 25) What's to know about sleep deprivation? Medical News Today

63 National Sleep Foundation NSF2015

64 Jeffrey M. Jones. (2013, December 19) In U.S., 40% Get Less Than Recommended Amount of Sleep. *Gallup*

65 National Institute of Neurological Disorders and Stroke (2018, July 6) Brain Basics: Understanding Sleep. National Institute of Health, 2

66 ibid, 5

Index